LADY

in

RED

LADY *in* RED

AN INTIMATE
PORTRAIT
of
NANCY REAGAN

SHEILA TATE

CROWN
FORUM
NEW YORK

Published in the United States by Crown Forum, an imprint of the Crown
Publishing Group, a division of Penguin Random House LLC, New York.
crownpublishing.com

CROWN FORUM with colophon is a registered trademark of Penguin
Random House LLC.

Photograph credits are located on page 237.

Library of Congress Cataloging-in-Publication Data has been applied for.

ISBN 978-1-5247-6219-3
Ebook ISBN 978-1-5247-6221-6

Printed in the United States of America

Jacket design by Alane Gianetti
Jacket photograph: Portrait of Nancy Davis Reagan by Aaron Shikler,
1987/White House Collection/White House Historical Association

10 9 8 7 6 5 4 3 2 1

First Edition

To John K. Youel Jr., my husband of twelve years, for his superhuman patience and his knowledge of how to fix my Epson printer and scanner. For his superb chauffeuring skills and his patience with Daisy, my yappy dog. Not to mention his surgical skills, which he still puts to occasional use in repairing various household items. And for forcing me onto the golf course a few times during the writing of this book to regain my equilibrium and sense of proportion.

To my children, Hager Patton and Courtney Manzel, and to their great spouses, Shannon and Kevin, and to my perfect grandchildren, Colin, Avery, Greyson, and Lily; to my amazing stepdaughters, Jennifer Tate Citron and Laura Tate Hudgins, and to their husbands, Jerry and Snow, and to their five wonderful children, Chloe and Eve Citron and Tate, Finley, and Sawyer Hudgins. Hager was my long-distance computer guru whose skills were invaluable; Courtney was my eagle-eyed legal authority who helped in a million ways.

To John's children, Ellen and Mahzer Ahmad and David and Chrissy Youel, and to John's four fun grandchildren, Jack, Maggie, Sophia, and Zakaria. Ellen performed a miracle—helping me find George Opfer, Nancy's lead Secret Service agent.

Contents

LADY

in

RED

Foreword

Nancy Reagan was truly one of the most loyal and protective spouses I have ever met in my ninety-three years. My dear friend Ronald Reagan could not have asked for a better partner. No matter the issue—politics, world affairs, inside White House gamesmanship—Nancy had his back. She and I tangled a time or two, and she could be a complicated person, but I always knew—even when we disagreed—that her motives were pure. It was never about her. It was about her beloved Ronnie. And for that she had my utmost respect.

—President George H.W. Bush
April 20, 2017

Introduction

One of the hardest things I ever had to do was to tell Nancy Reagan I was leaving the White House. After working for her for more than four years as her press secretary, I reluctantly decided it was time to leave government service and to return to a more normal life, if that's the right way to describe the public relations business. My government service over those four years had involved so much sacrifice and inconvenience. Not for me; for my husband and children. Because my schedule as press secretary was subject to change at a moment's notice, we, my husband and I, realized that for four years we had never been able to entertain our friends. I missed many of my children's school activities, but they missed their mother being at home at night, making dinner and talking over the day. It felt like the right time to say goodbye.

Still, it was difficult to give the news to the First Lady, with whom I had worked so closely and whom I had come to know and admire greatly.

We were standing in the middle of the private living room in the residence when I blurted out my news with tears in my eyes. I told her how much it hurt to leave. "Thank you, Mrs. Reagan," I said, "for allowing me the honor of working for you." She walked up next to me and hugged me. We talked for a while and she suggested it was high time I started calling her "Nancy." I would do so for the next thirty years.

The story of how I came to be Nancy Reagan's White House press secretary is one of happenstance, Irish luck, and a well-connected boss.

I grew up in the Virginia suburbs of Washington, the second of five children. My dad was a communications attorney in DC; my mother was a traditional homemaker. In 1960, after graduating from Falls Church High, I was off to college at Duquesne University in Pittsburgh, where I majored in journalism—the who, what, when, where, and why school of journalism—and then began my career working at various public relations agencies. That was work I loved. I married and divorced; by 1979 I was back in Falls Church with two wonderful children, ages six and nine.

Two years later, two major developments changed my life. I married a wonderful fellow named Bill Tate and Nancy Reagan gave me a job.

Bob Gray headed up the Hill and Knowlton Washington office where I worked. He became communications director of the Reagan Bush campaign, taking several staff members with him to join the effort while I stayed behind to run a large portion of our business. The only political work I did was early in the primaries when I made evening calls as a volunteer at the phone bank asking for donations to Texas governor John Connally's campaign for the presidency.

After Ronald Reagan won the election in 1980, Bob Gray called and asked me to send him a copy of my résumé. He was aware of a position for which he felt I was well qualified. He said he couldn't tell me what it was but that it was right up my alley. The next thing I knew, within hours, I was asked to be at Blair House that evening at 6:00 p.m. I had walked by Blair House, the official White House guesthouse, too many times to count but had never been inside. It was and is on Pennsylvania Avenue, across the street from the White House.

In between that call and my arrival, I got dressed in a navy-blue suit and realized that the only nice heels I had were a mess. Off to the shoe repair shop where I begged the repairman to shine them while I waited.

When I checked in with the receptionist at Blair House, she motioned for me to sit down and told me someone would come for me shortly. I began noticing people I'd just seen on television walking through that room—General Alexander Haig, who had been appointed secretary of state, and National Security Advisor Dick Allen. The room itself was a lovely old-fashioned parlor, and I started thinking about how this house had functioned as the White House for a period of time when Harry Truman was president while he was having the now famous Truman balcony installed on the south side of the White House. And the attempt on his life while he was there.

After a wait of about fifteen minutes, Peter McCoy— Nancy's first and by my measure best chief of staff—came out to meet me, introduced himself, and ushered me upstairs to a second-floor room. I had figured out the potential job must be the press secretary job by the time I met Nancy. Bob Gray had told me that I would be meeting Nancy Reagan and that the job was in the East Wing. I had read the negative press coverage she received about wanting the Carters to move out of the White House early capped off by a story that she slept with a "tiny little gun" when Ronnie was out of town. I remember wondering if this would be an impossible job.

There she was, Nancy Reagan, in real life, standing waiting for me. She was, I recall, wearing a green wool dress. After greeting me, she said, "I have been looking forward to meeting you after reading your résumé." I said, "I am thrilled to be here and to have the chance to meet you in person."

We sat and managed to have a good discussion—I kept my shaky hands under my legs for most of the meeting—and she told me then she wanted to find a way to become involved in the youth drug abuse issue. She asked me to tell her about my experience and the clients I'd had. As I look back on that meeting, which lasted less than an hour, I would describe her as reserved; I could tell she was listening carefully to whatever I said and evaluating me.

I do remember wondering if drug abuse was the right issue for her—I thought perhaps it was too dark for a First Lady. What drew her to this cause? And wondering whether she could have any credibility in discussing it. Had she ever confronted drug abuse in her own family? I wanted to ask her so many questions but I held my tongue. As I took my leave I said to her, "Mrs. Reagan, it has been a pleasure to meet you and if I can do anything for this exciting new administration,

I would be honored." She smiled and simply said, "Thank you so much for coming."

She pointedly never mentioned exactly what job she was talking with me about which really confused me; I left wondering why we didn't get down to brass tacks. I assumed my chances for the job were slim, not having worked on the Reagan campaign, so I was pleasantly surprised when Peter McCoy followed up and asked me to meet with a few other people. And I learned the reason for the lack of specificity in my conversation with Nancy. She had initially hired a society reporter, Robin Orr, from California to be her press secretary. It was not a good fit. When Nancy realized she needed someone who was more familiar with politics and the DC press, she had decided to replace her. She had not yet notified Robin and didn't want her to find out about her replacement without advance notice. On the other hand, she knew it was important to have a successor lined up before the news broke.

The following week, at her request, I met individually with Mike Deaver, the much-heralded Reagan aide; Tish Baldridge, the delightful former social secretary to Jackie Kennedy; Nancy Reynolds, the personable Reagan staffer from California who became head of the Bendix Corporation's Washington office, and Jim Brady, the "Bear" who was just named President Reagan's press secretary. Nancy and Tish were helping Mrs. Reagan assemble her staff during the transition. All those meetings were at Blair House, except the meeting with Jim, which was at the Transition Office.

The day I met Jim—and instantly became a member of his fan club—he told me the process had narrowed to two people and that he was voting for me. That was apparently what tipped the scale in my favor because that night Nancy called and offered me the position. I accepted immediately because by then I had thought through the pros and cons and decided I wanted the job. She said it would be announced on Monday. It was ten days before the inauguration. The *Washington Post* had other plans, however. I was awakened by a late-night call on Saturday evening; Elisabeth Bumiller wanted me to confirm that I was going to be Nancy Reagan's press secretary. I refused to confirm it and the *Post* printed their story anyway. I never did learn who their sources were. But I called the Transition Office to give them a heads-up on the call.

On Monday I made my way to the Transition Office and found Barbara Walters sitting next to my desk. She'd traveled to Washington because she wanted to be the first reporter to ask for and get the first interview with Nancy Reagan. I was impressed and I lobbied on her behalf; I considered her one of the best news reporters in the business. She didn't get the first interview, but she did get an interview. You may recall her famous question: "Mrs. Reagan, if you were a tree, what kind of a tree would you be?"

While Barbara and I were talking that first day, a secretary handed me a pile of about a hundred call slips from reporters around the world. As soon as she left, I began the grueling job of returning each of those calls. It took the better part of the week to catch up with the backlog. From that day through all my years at the White House, I returned every call before I went home at night. The only exceptions to that rule were two: I did not return calls from the *National Enquirer* or Kitty Kelley.

Those first days at the Transition Office were exhausting, both physically and mentally. I vividly recall driving home and throwing myself into bed, wondering if I would ever get things under control. Little did I realize at the time that as the years passed Nancy Reagan would play a central role in my life, not just as my "boss" but ultimately as my friend and confidante.

And then, on Inauguration Day, we walked into the White House for the first time. My first White House friend, Jim Brady, took me under his wing from the start. He and Larry Speakes, his deputy and my former colleague at Hill and Knowlton, invited me to sit in on the West Wing Press Office's daily 8:00 a.m. meeting. This ensured that the two separate press operations—East and West—never stepped on each other's events. It seemed like such a basic management decision; I was surprised to hear it was the first time East and West press secretaries met daily to coordinate their schedules. Jim was an enormous help to me in winning a number of internal power struggles and he was a formidable ally. For instance, in the first few weeks, I went to Jim after running into resistance to my media plan for our first official state dinner. A social secretary had overstepped her authority and changed my carefully developed "photo ops" for the press who would cover it. Jim took one look at the inappropriate changes and pushed me toward Mike Deaver's office while muttering to himself, "What in the 'blank' do they think we have these dinners for?. . . They are for the press." That was his direct way of saying that these events were organized to convey to the rest of the world the significant relationship each guest country had with the United States. We needed the press coverage to achieve important diplomatic objectives. Jim helped me get my plan returned to its original order and I became his biggest fan. And could that man make chili.

Just a few years ago I was honored to speak at Jim's memorial; I will mourn his loss to the day I die. What a magnificent human being. Did I mention he was the chili king of Washington?

Before I even became familiar with all the staff and their offices in the White House, Nancy's schedule quickly filled up with events and travels. I was expected to travel with her if she had any public events on the schedule. We spent hours talking about our experiences, our plans. She used to poke fun at me about all the time I spent on the plane doing needlepoint. She asked, "What do you do with all the things you've made?" I told her she was next on the list to get a needlepoint present. I also told her I loved needlepoint because it helped you think in an orderly fashion; and almost always I was thinking through the next media event as I sewed. I was "embroidering" that explanation.

When I think about it, I realize that seldom a day went by without our talking on the phone if not in person. And it was unusual not to talk multiple times each day. Once, as my family and I enjoyed a vacation week at Stone Harbor, New Jersey, in a beach house without a phone—remember, this was the early '80s and no one had cell phones until years later—the local police drove up to our cottage in a marked police car and told me to call the White House. I walked a block to the nearest phone booth to talk with her. I often wondered what the neighbors must have thought when they saw me more than once in that phone booth.

Over all the years I knew her, I never considered writing a book about Nancy Reagan.

I did receive occasional publishing offers for a few years after I left the White House; I refused those requests because I felt strongly that to do my job properly, Nancy had to entrust me with a good deal of personal information. That information belonged to her, not to me. I also felt that she had not finished the "story" of her life and she still had many years of history to make. But I changed my mind the year after I said one last painful goodbye to her at her memorial service in California on March 11, 2016, five days after her death.

At that service so many friends gathered and we talked about our times with Nancy and how different she was from the caricature created by the press. I wish all Americans could have known her as I did. This book is my personal effort to try to convey the real, substantial, thoughtful woman I knew and whose friendship I valued deeply. I realized after her death I had so many memories that would be lost to history if I didn't put pen to paper.

This book is filled with visuals that I think the reader will enjoy. When you work at the White House, you seldom think of the historic value of the ceremonies you witnessed and the documents you dropped carelessly onto your desk afterward; you're always too busy, going in so many different directions. I was even surprised to find so many handwritten notes from her all these years later. And wonderful pictures. I was part—a small part, but a part—of that history. And the Nancy Reagan I knew has never been adequately described.

On one of my visits to the Reagan home in California, Nancy gave me a packet of her favorite photos of her husband

and some of them as a couple. She asked me to handle the press when he died and to give reporters the photos and encourage them to use them. I like two of the photos the best: one is the two of them on the dock of their little lake at their ranch, taken from behind; the other is them in their canoe.

When this opportunity arose to write a book, I could almost hear Nancy saying *Do it, Sheila*. And now here I am getting ready to tell you about the Nancy I came to know, admire, and whose friendship I cherished. She was no cardboard cutout. She was sometimes complicated; she could get on your nerves. But who couldn't? Sometimes she made me mentally roll my eyes. It is true that she did love the phone as reporters frequently reported—as if it were a flaw—and her calls were never short. Some of those calls came at inconvenient times, but looking back now I treasure them all. She could be stubborn and sometimes her judgment wasn't perfect. She was a human being. Imagine that.

At the lunch after her funeral I asked my friend Mark Weinberg, former press officer for President Reagan, what he would most miss about her. Turns out we both had the same answer: we would miss hearing her voice. That distinctive Nancy voice. And Mark could even mimic her voice so well it would often fool me. It was and still is hard to imagine when the phone rings she will never be on the other end of the line.

In the course of writing this book, I have had the privilege of talking to so many friends of Nancy's and old friends of mine: coworkers in the Reagan White House; some Democrats as well as Republicans; reporters who covered her; children of old friends. Each person added a piece to the portrait of Nancy I wanted to share.

I begin at the beginning: the first rocky year in the White House, 1981, from the transition to the details of Nancy's refurbishment of the White House and the press criticism that went with it. And as painful as it still is, I revisit the assassination attempt on President Reagan and the First Lady's grief that lasted through Jim Brady's death thirty-five years later.

And I take you behind the scenes to introduce you to Nancy's top-secret preparations when she appeared onstage dressed as a bag lady to win over the press critics at the Gridiron Dinner, and then to go on the road to begin a never-ending campaign to fight youth drug abuse.

I promise you will get to know her better, and some of what I write may surprise you. I spent many hours discussing the possible roots of her protectiveness with some of her family and friends. What I learned from her brother astonished even me. And, in my opinion, her perfectionism was something to be admired.

And nothing was more magical than the Reagan White House at Christmas. I go into great detail—both the exhausting schedule and the exhilarating moment during one special Christmas when Nancy introduced Amie Garrison, a five-year-old girl in desperate need of a liver transplant, to the unexpecting White House press corps. It's an incredible story.

I give you a glimpse into Nancy's artsy side and her special affinity for young artists.

You'll also learn about Nancy's growing self-confidence in public speaking, from her timid first appearance before the East Wing press in early 1981 to the last speech she gave as First Lady—to children at Boys Town. That speech is powerful proof of how much Nancy had grown and changed; how much she'd come to recognize the power for good she possessed; and how comfortable she became in telling emotional personal stories in public.

While I never thought of Nancy as a diplomat, she was, in fact, a superb one. She made real friends all across the globe. I devote considerable attention to details of not only her impact on world leaders but also her personal diplomacy, which helped save lives. I dare you to read about Brett and Diana Halvorson without feeling a lump in your throat.

It was a special honor to write about Nancy's security, especially because it revolves around George Opfer, Nancy's lead agent for the first six years of the Reagan presidency. George had always refused to talk publicly about Nancy before with anyone, but he trusted me to treat his recollections properly. He also entrusted me with the notes Nancy wrote to him during those six years. George epitomized the professional Secret Service officer, the best of the best. And I know Nancy agreed with me; she put her life in his hands. Literally. And two other members of Nancy's security, Joe Sullivan and John Barletta, talked with me at length about their memorable experiences on Nancy's detail.

Nancy had a distinctive style. She was a classic; President Reagan said she never threw anything away. Mainly because none of her clothes ever went out of style. You will learn all about her fashion sense from her off-the-rack press secretary, so take what I say with a grain of salt. She favored the deep red color that came to be known as Reagan red. And that's why this book's title and cover design were so easy to conceive.

I had some fun revealing a closely held secret among White House staffers: a president's wife—no matter who—is a very convenient excuse for saying no to a request. It's the staff's easy way out and I am not without sin. You'll see.

Nancy's relationship with the press was my area of professional expertise. A good deal of silly gossip passed for news in those days and I was always batting false stories down. Part of the problem was solved, or at least mitigated, as the press came to know her better. But it was a never-ending challenge. The seriousness of her drug abuse campaign won over some reporters; her growing self-confidence in her interactions with them also was helpful.

Nancy was my boss and I always respected the way she worked with me. She said she would always take my calls, no matter how many. That was critical to my ability to perform my job. She never went back on that promise. When our professional relationship grew into a real friendship, I found I also admired her private side. I recall the wonderful experiences of traveling with Nancy; what an amazing friend she was. And I am particularly proud to share staff memories from about a dozen of those who consider themselves lucky to have been on her team. Many are very funny.

It seemed most appropriate to me to close by remembering what brought us all together to begin with, the presidency of Ronald Reagan. And finally, to say goodbye to Nancy. A sad time, for sure, but when you read about Digby, the dog, you'll find it impossible not to smile.

In the course of writing this book, I learned a great deal about Nancy that even I did not know. I dearly hope that I have brought her voice to this book, that I help the reader come to better know and appreciate a woman who deserves our respect and admiration. I have the distinct feeling that she is looking over my shoulder, especially when I need to correct something. She was, after all, a perfectionist.

1

Elegance and Style

My first assignment in December 1980, as the newly named press secretary for Nancy Reagan, was to entrust one of the Reagan advance men with the highly confidential assignment of driving to New York City to pick up the final glossy sketches of Nancy's inaugural wardrobe. Now, thirty-eight years later, I am free to unmask my accomplice. Mark Hatfield, son of Senator Mark Hatfield of Oregon, took on the assignment. Mark Jr., my hero, did not disappoint.

When he returned to our nation's capital, he met me in the parking lot of transition headquarters where we transferred the contraband from his trunk to mine. Sounds a bit like Deep Throat, doesn't it?

It really was important to keep those designs secret until Nancy wore those outfits. There had been instances in past presidencies where this kind of information was leaked in advance. It puts a real damper on the excitement of the day. I believe the worst example was when Lynda Bird Johnson was marrying Chuck Robb; drawings of her wedding dress designed by Geoffrey Beene were leaked to *Women's Wear Daily* before Lynda's special, historic White House wedding took place.

Nancy's outfit on Inauguration Day—a red crepe day dress with a red twill coat and hat—was created by American designer Adolfo. Its brilliant red hue quickly became known as Reagan red. She favored that color for the rest of her life. It became an essential part of her style.

I thought it was the perfect color for her. Not that she consulted me on that subject! After all, less than ten days earlier I had been working at a large public relations firm's Washington office, directing national publicity efforts in favor of continued regulation of the trucking industry. I'd never even heard of Adolfo before.

Shortly before the January 20, 1981, swearing-in and at some time during the luncheon in the Capitol, our new president, Ronald Reagan, was able to announce that our American heroes—held hostage for 444 days in Iran—had been released and had just cleared Iranian airspace on their way home. As an added grace note, he dispatched former president Jimmy Carter, who worked tirelessly to bring them home, to meet the hostages as they reached safety.

All of America celebrated. The National Christmas Tree on the Ellipse between the White House and the Washington Monument was lit that night in celebration for the first time since they had been taken hostage. That evening the Reagans danced at eight inaugural balls, Nancy in a glittering white gown and gorgeous satin coat designed by James Galanos, another top American designer. The president, by the way, wore a tuxedo. I do not know who designed it. It was black.

Those balls were packed with ecstatic Republicans from across the country. I was present at the ball held at the Capital Hilton where the coat check line snaked around the block. In truth, it was no more glamorous than a high school prom, except we did have alcohol. In paper cups. Funny the things one remembers. I also remember that it was so overcrowded that every foray onto the dance floor ended up with some man stepping on my feet.

The ballroom came alive when the new president and First Lady arrived. Everyone knew they were witnessing the beginning of an exciting new presidential term. I was thrilled to be even a small part of it. It was one of the few presidential events that I would not have to work; the West Wing presidential advance people took charge. I got to be a witness to history.

Nancy's inaugural gown, in keeping with long-standing tradition, was eventually donated to the Smithsonian. I grew up in the DC suburbs and for as long as I can remember, the wing of the American History Museum that houses its gown collection has always been the most popular exhibit at the Smithsonian. Folks at the Smithsonian confirmed that fact when I was working on the details of Nancy's donation. The oldest inaugural gown in the museum's collection dates from 1829 and belonged to Andrew Johnson's niece. The oldest First Lady's gown in the Smithsonian collection—not part of an inauguration— belonged to none other than Martha Washington.

* * *

Nancy Reagan really was an American classic. Her style and grace has held up through the decades. It took care, thought, and planning to be the First Lady, and she understood that her image was important.

Imagine having to attend multiple public events nearly every day. Imagine at least twenty of those events every year are formal in nature. And imagine having the media documenting, photographing, and commenting on every outfit you wear.

Some First Ladies have been publicly adjudged to be frumpy; others to have poor taste. And lord help you if you wore something too frequently; the style press would not be kind to you.

Nancy organized her wardrobe to keep track of when each outfit was worn. Other First Ladies had also found this tactic helpful, but I'd never seen it before and found it amazing. A tag hung from each outfit listing the dates and events to which it had been worn.

Sometimes, her outfit made the news when we didn't intend it. When Nancy wore her fur coat in public one cold winter evening, we received bags of critical mail. Almost all of it was generated by animal rights activists and it was pretty ugly.

And once, at a congressional wives' reception on the Hill one rainy day, Susan Watters from *Women's Wear Daily* insisted I find out from Nancy how to describe the vivid quilted purple outfit she was wearing. I slipped into the front of the receiving line and quietly asked Nancy how to describe it. She said, "It's a purple rain outfit." I returned to Susan with that information, but the press was not yet satisfied. Another reporter had a follow-up: she asked me to interrupt Nancy once more and find out what kind of fur trim was on the collar. I lost my patience and said something to the effect of "It's a dead animal." I learned quickly that one did not make light references to expired furry creatures connected to First Ladies. My mail was highly negative to put it mildly. One said: "I have seen your type; your vacant stare; your empty eyes." My personal favorite letter came addressed to "King Ronald, Queen Nancy and Princess Sheila." I was royalty!

By far Nancy's greatest volume of mail during my years of service dealt with fashion. Nancy generally looked great in whatever she wore and that was what a lot of Americans were interested in.

Nancy made only one major style misstep as First Lady that I can recall: the infamous knickers.

The Reagans were on a European trip in early June 1982, and while in Paris, they attended a party in honor of François Mitterrand at the American ambassador's residence. We were all enjoying the evening when the press in attendance suddenly perked up. Helen Thomas of UPI pulled me aside and said, in her serious, authoritative, rather piercing Helen Thomas voice, "What the hell is she wearing?" I realized that I had failed to find out in advance the details of her outfit. There was such a stir among the press corps that I had to pull Nancy aside and ask for the details.

The knickers were a James Galanos creation—a black chiffon skirt over rhinestone-studded black satin knickers. Those knickers were publicized worldwide. I regret never asking Nancy why she chose to wear that outfit. I suspect she wanted to make a big fashion statement in Paris, the center of haute couture. The sensation, thankfully, was short-lived.

* * *

January 20 is the constitutionally required date for routine presidential inaugurations. In 1985, that happened to be on a Sunday that was also Super Bowl Sunday. So it was decided that to comply with the law, there would be a private swearing in at the White House on Sunday, January 20, and then a public/ceremonial swearing in at the Capitol on Monday, January 21, to be followed by the traditional parade and balls at hotels across town. Initially, Mike Deaver did not want press coverage of the private swearing in, because he did not want to detract from the next day's extravaganza. He proposed that there be an official White House photo release of the actual swearing in, after which the Reagans and Bushes would briefly appear on the North Portico for a picture together. The press objected vigorously, and Mike wisely relented. There was a pool of reporters and photographers on the State Floor when Reagan was sworn in on the Grand Staircase before a small audience of family, Cabinet, bipartisan congressional leaders, friends, and senior staff. True to form, Mrs. Reagan wore red and beamed as she held the Bible while Chief Justice Warren E. Burger administered the oath of office to her husband.

That Sunday was the coldest anyone could remember in Washington history, and as the day went on, the temperatures dropped. Way down. So much so, the Reagans reluctantly accepted the Inaugural Committee's recommendation to move all events indoors. Due to the extreme cold weather, an evening concert for Sunday and all of the next day's outdoor inaugural events, specifically the swearing in ceremony at the Capitol and the parade on Pennsylvania Avenue, were moved inside. Mrs. Reagan was especially worried about the danger to the young people playing in bands during the parade because exposure to the cold—especially to those playing metal musical instruments—could cause injury. I remember standing on the North Portico of the White House and shivering during a brief TV interview to explain the decision to move that evening's and the next day's events inside. After less than a minute I had to end the interview because my eyelids had frozen shut!

On Monday, January 21, Reagan was sworn in again, inside the Capitol, only this time Mrs. Reagan surprised everyone and wore a light blue suit, complete with a matching hat, to the ceremony. After this second swearing in, the president delivered his full inaugural address; he and Mrs. Reagan attended the traditional postceremony luncheon in the Capitol, and then they went out to the Capital Center in Landover, Maryland, for a makeup concert and parade with people who had been scheduled to perform outdoors. The Reagans wanted to tell the people how sorry they were that Mother Nature changed the carefully laid plans and how much they appreciated everyone's flexibility, efforts, and support. Admittedly, the event was hastily arranged, which I think may have unsettled Mrs. Reagan a bit. She was supposed to say a few words and then introduce her husband to speak. She delivered her remarks perfectly and then sat down—*without introducing him*! After an awkward silence, she realized her mistake and rushed back to the podium where she introduced the man she called "my roommate."

Later that evening they attended eleven inaugural balls.

When I was thinking about this chapter, Donald Trump was on his first overseas trip as president. Several times I found myself looking up at Melania on TV, beautiful and dignified. And then I heard repeated commentary on how Jackie Kennedy, Nancy Reagan, and Melania Trump were the most stylish First Ladies we've had. Each different but each representing us well. I agree. I think Nancy would have been so pleased to be in such good company.

2

The Boss

Nothing in this world is more important for a press secretary's reputation and credibility than his or her access to the boss.

Nancy told me early in our working relationship that she didn't want to be surprised by something I'd said to the media, and that she would always be available to me if I needed her reaction to or guidance about a question from the press. Sometimes I tested the limits. There were days when she got as many as eight or ten calls from me. She always gave me the time I needed. We were a good team. She made me look good. And I did my best to provide equal service.

Nancy never gossiped with staff. We had a professional relationship with her. We met together monthly—the chief of staff, social secretary, projects director, and press secretary—in her upstairs office overlooking Pennsylvania Avenue, to focus on the details of her next thirty- to sixty-day schedule and to finalize our plans. Those meetings often lasted several hours. She rarely made any adjustments to our recommended calendar. Which may be why we were so surprised years later to learn about her dependence on astrology to guide the development of the president's schedule. She definitely was not relying on astrology to plan her own schedule.

In planning Nancy's schedule, we quickly came to understand she always wanted to know if others were speaking at the same event. If so, she wanted staff coordination with the staff of other speakers to make sure everyone's remarks were relevant and avoided duplication.

And, of course, she was equally desirous of knowing the weather forecast for any trip. She was always worried about the weather and being cold. A recurring theme!

Muffie Brandon, her social secretary, described Nancy as very thorough and sometimes a bit demanding but always with her concern focused on her husband's success and well-being. "She held herself to very high standards and worked ceaselessly to achieve her goals. She expected nothing less from those of us who worked for her."

Ann Wrobleski says she always thinks of Nancy as the "reluctant" boss or maybe "unlikely" boss.

Although she had a public life before the White House as a movie actress and as First Lady of California, she'd never had a staff. While she borrowed people like Nancy Reynolds and Carol McCain to help her on the campaign trail or for important events, for the most part, her team was herself and her housekeeper.

All that changed in Washington. Nancy Reynolds ran

the First Lady's office during the transition and did much of the hiring. But the day after the inaugural Nancy found herself with a chief of staff, social secretary, press secretary, project director, scheduler, personal assistant, and their attendant deputies and assistants. Suddenly she had a big team and we all wanted her time, attention, and, most importantly, direction.

We all had questions that needed answers so that we could get on with the work we were hired to do.

Ann Wrobleski had worked on Capitol Hill for two senators and a congressman and been a spokesman for two statewide candidates in Florida. "Like everyone else on her staff, I was used to both taking and giving instructions. Nancy seemed more comfortable making suggestions rather than giving directions.

"That said, I found Nancy to be more thoughtful than my previous bosses and also more likely to ask the next question. So, for example, 'Can I sit with the children?' was followed by 'Where will their parents sit?' Most political figures are happy with an answer to the first question as they usually are all about them.

"Nancy was also always well prepared. She did her homework, practiced her remarks, and was mindful of the purpose of every event."

Ann remembered one anecdote in particular:

The first head of government to visit the Reagans was Prime Minister Edward Seaga of Jamaica. He and his wife came for a state lunch on January 28 and Nancy and the president were outside the Diplomatic Entrance to welcome them.

Nancy warmly greeted the prime minister and then turned to extend the same greeting to the woman she assumed was his wife. Instead, the woman was a U.S. Foreign Service officer who accompanied the Jamaican guests. The woman quickly introduced Nancy to the real Mrs. Seaga, correcting her diplomatic error as graciously as she could.

Ann says Nancy was determined to never make that mistake again and from that day forward she received her own briefing materials from the National Security Council and the State Department, which she studied carefully.

Ann and I worked as a team, creating and organizing events for Nancy that had the substance Ann insisted upon and the news value I demanded. To this day, we remain close friends. One of her twin boys (now young men working on Capitol Hill) is my godson. And we attended her daughter's beautiful wedding several years ago in the North Carolina mountains.

3

The New First Lady

Nancy Davis Reagan came to Washington with her husband, the former California governor. She had always been devoted to Ronald Reagan; he came first. He always talked about how wonderful it was to come home to Nancy at the end of each day. She likewise came first as far as he was concerned. When they married, his friends were hers and she brought more friends into the fold as the years went by. The Bloomingdales, the Annenbergs, the Wicks, and many more. Life was good and uncomplicated. All the Californians came with them to Washington to celebrate the inauguration of their great friend. New York friends joined them.

And the press had a field day, contrasting the West Coast invaders and their ostentatious lifestyle with the current financial malaise of the country.

Nancy was quoted (by some anonymous source) as wishing the Carters would move out of the White House early, presumably so she could begin to settle in. So, as you can imagine, Nancy was not viewed sympathetically as she came to live in Washington.

Nancy's initial focus was on creating a comfortable environment for her husband and herself as she had always done in their previous homes.

When the Reagans moved into the White House in 1981, she recognized the visible wear and tear on that wonderful historic home and office; there were cracks in the plaster, mold, chipped paint, and worn floors and carpets. She wanted to completely restore it, not just to make it comfortable for them but to make it a source of pride for America. She considered the White House to be the people's house and she wanted to make it shine.

But there is a quandary that every first family faces when they arrive: the amount Congress allots to first families for improvements when they first take up residence in the White House is relatively small. The one-time-only allowance has fluctuated over the years, increasing to $50,000 in 1925; it was raised to $100,000 in 1999. As a result, most families before the Reagans made modest improvements with their $50,000 stipends and the building's basic maintenance got deferred. Over the years that led to erosion in plumbing, outdated electrical systems, and mold. The huge antique doors on the State Floor, where most official events were held, had not been refinished since the Truman family walked the halls in the late 1940s.

Nancy decided to face the need for major restoration head-on. The Reagans turned back the federal stipend and she raised close to one million dollars in private contributions to refurbish the White House.

Twenty years earlier Jackie Kennedy had set up a volunteer committee of antique enthusiasts to help her restore the White House. She also created the White House Historical Association in order to accept private donations. The smartest thing she did, to my mind, was involve *Life* magazine early, using it as a forum to explain and preview her plans, building popular support in advance. She was wise beyond her years.

Nancy felt that she needed to approach her restoration differently, both because the media was not sympathetic to her and because we were in the midst of a painful economic recession. She did not want to preview her plans; she wanted to showcase them when the work was complete.

Nancy brought in experts to assess the electrical and plumbing needs hidden behind the plaster walls as well as the cosmetic aspects of both the residence and the State Floor.

Friends of the Reagans in Oklahoma started raising private funds and they raised so much so fast from Oklahomans that the fund-raising effort was stopped almost before it began. That effort was criticized because most of the money came from oil and gas interests, the first and most logical prospects from which to raise funds in oil-rich Oklahoma.

And as all modern First Ladies have done, Nancy brought in her favorite decorator, Ted Graber, to walk through the White House furniture warehouses with her, selecting antique furnishings to complement the Reagans' personal furniture from California.

The result, completed within the first year, was a beautifully restored and furnished residence that would make future presidential families comfortable for years to come. The work on the State Floor would provide future presidents a dignified venue to entertain world leaders, and all without cost to the taxpayers. The actual restoration work in the private quarters was essentially complete before I was able to view it; the residence was off-limits to staff while it was under restoration. When I did get to see the restoration, I have to admit I was enchanted. It was a beautiful, comfortable home with many of the Reagans' personal effects adding to its hominess. Years later, after George and Barbara Bush were living there, Mrs. Bush told me that every day she was there she thanked Nancy Reagan for the work she had done.

On top of the restoration and redecorating, Nancy had ordered a new set of White House china. She called me to come to the State Dining Room one morning in the early summer. She had just approved a sample place setting of the new Reagan (red) china and wanted me to see it firsthand. I asked for permission to have the White House photographer photograph the setting for use when we released it. My first instinct was that we needed to release the information as soon as possible because it surely would leak. The Lenox china factory was gearing up to produce the china, exposing this information to any number of artisans involved in the process. Mike Deaver overruled me and to this day I think that was a mistake. He wanted us to keep it under wraps until the Christmas holidays when the press would be more likely to write balanced stories. I was next to certain the story would not hold. Sorry to say, I was right.

Within weeks, Maureen Santini of the Associated Press had the story, and I had to scramble. Thank goodness Nancy had given me the chance to develop press materials or it would have been worse.

The cost was $209,000 for a service for 250 guests, entirely paid for by a private foundation. But we got no credit for that. The press was in what we called a "feeding frenzy" and no effort to communicate a more fulsome background story could break through the cacophony. Even my attempt to focus on facts like this—Eleanor Roosevelt ordered a new china service during the Depression and it was paid for by the Department of the Interior!—were paid any mind. Sadly, the china story had leaked to the Associated Press on the same day that ketchup was certified as a vegetable in the school lunch program by the Department of Agriculture. No reporter could pass up a "spicy" comparison like that.

When the work on the White House was complete, Nancy and I spent considerable time weighing the options for press coverage. *Architectural Digest* won first reporting rights. To us, it was a publication worthy of treating the Reagan restoration with the importance it deserved. Of course, that inflamed the insular political press corps in Washington where the prevailing view was that anything occurring at the White House had to be reported first by White House reporters.

Taken together in the first year of her tenure as First Lady, all this—new china, restoration work—created an image of Nancy as a brittle, uncaring, acquisitive socialite; that wasn't accurate but it was our fault.

Nancy took the media criticism because she knew she had helped preserve the White House for another fifty years. As her press secretary, I wondered if the press frenzy on these issues would ever diminish.

And then President Reagan held a routine press conference several weeks after the china frenzy began. When asked about the new china, he took this issue head-on. He said something to the effect that all this fuss over "dishes" for the White House was silly; it made the press look foolish. That shaming was all it took to make the press corps move on to other stories. God love Ronald Reagan, riding to Nancy's rescue.

The Reagans were determined to showcase the White House by hosting state dinners for heads of state from around the world. In their first term, they held thirty-two official state dinners as well as restored to the official calendar the formal Diplomatic Reception, previously an annual event that was very important to the ambassadors from every country. Those new "dishes" got quite a workout.

The first state dinner was on February 26, 1981, given in honor of Margaret Thatcher.

I recently listened to White House social secretary Muffie Brandon Cabot's oral history at the Reagan Library where she explained the incredible detail that goes into planning each state dinner and how important every detail was to Nancy. For instance, Muffie found out that Mrs. Thatcher loved anemones, so they were the colorful centerpiece on every table. And every table at the dinner was covered in green silk tablecloths because green was Mrs. Thatcher's favorite color. Maggie was touched.

I vividly remember having to ask the president, after the dinner but before the entertainment started, to let me borrow his index card on which he had written his toast. Several reporters were at odds with something they thought he said in the toast and needed to verify it. As he pulled it from his pocket he said, "Okay, Sheila, but be sure to return it to me because I have to turn it in to the folks who keep files on these things." His concern for the "folks" who were counting on him to return his index card for the archives was not unusual. That was the way he conducted himself. I reviewed the toast for the reporters who had not heard it correctly and immediately returned the index card to the president.

My routine for these state dinners never changed. I only had a few long gowns so I alternated wearing them. Nobody noticed my attire anyway. I always called Nancy the day of the event to get the details of her gown for the press. The social office always furnished my press office with the guest list and the menu, again for me to background the press. The dinners were held in the State Dining Room with fifteen tables of eight, allowing room for the waiters to move about easily. Often the "Strolling Strings," a graceful line of uniformed army violinists, walked through the room at one point to add to the glamor of the evening. They were magical. After dinner, guests were invited to have coffee in the color rooms, the Green, Blue, and Red Rooms between the State Dining Room and the East Room.

During coffee, I brought the social writers—usually four or five reporters—into the Grand Foyer and they were allowed to mingle with the guests for a few minutes before everyone was escorted into the East Room for the entertainment. I kept an "eagle eye" on each of those reporters and made sure I could hear what they were asking our guests. As good reporters they were always looking for a way to corner the president to ask a few questions about current events. My job was to minimize the time they had him cornered. Again, I listened and helped ensure we made no news during the evening by steering the conversation as best I could. The press was then escorted to a roped-off section reserved for television cameras, photographers, and writers. The entertainment following Mrs. Thatcher's dinner featured the vocalist George Benson and the Dance Theatre of Harlem. I remember cringing every time one of the dancers leapt into the air onstage and only missed the chandelier by inches.

Fittingly, the very last Reagan state dinner on November 18, 1988, was also in honor of Margaret Thatcher with whom Ronald Reagan had such a strong friendship, the fifty-third dinner of his presidency.

December was the only month we never held a state dinner. When you learn about the frenzy that is Christmas at the White House, you will understand why.

Muffie remembers when the fabulous Ella Fitzgerald came to perform at one of the early state dinners that first year. According to Muffie, "She was shaking with nervousness and I led her downstairs to the quiet and seclusion of a small reception room where she wanted to 'warm up' for her performance after dinner." During the dinner in the State Dining Room the president got Muffie's attention and asked her, "What is that singing going on?" Turns out the new air-conditioning vents were wide open and the president and his guests, in the glow of the lovingly refurbished State Floor, got to enjoy a preview of Ella's fabulous vocalizing.

I recall one evening when Muffie herself was nervous. It was at a state dinner later in 1981 honoring the prime minister of Israel, Menachem Begin, where we employed a kosher chef stationed in a van outside the back door of the kitchen. The meals were coming out of the van much too slowly so Muffie stood by the dumbwaiter that carried those meals to the State Floor, urging on the rabbi who was holding up each meal in order to bless it. Her exact words accompanied by appropriate arm gestures: "Move it, move it!"

Muffie also has vivid memories of a famous male vocalist at another state dinner that first year. He shall remain nameless. He was described politely by Muffie as "in his cups." Apparently he decided to stroll down the center aisle as he warbled (and wobbled) away. He came upon Barbara Bush and he tried to sit in her lap. Barbara stood up just in time to keep him standing.

* * *

Just when I thought we had passed all the initial controversies, a new issue revealed itself.

When news broke that Nancy had been wearing gowns "loaned" to her by famous designers, Fred Fielding, White House legal counsel, became my new best friend. What was common practice in Hollywood was a miniscandal in Washington. Eventually I announced that those gowns, still in Nancy's possession, were being donated to museums. That put an end to the story. But it was one more damaging incident that created a great deal of angst in the East Wing.

* * *

Midway into the first year, Prince Charles and Lady Diana were married in the wedding of the century. The Reagans were invited, of course, but the president was still recovering from the bullet wound he suffered in the attempt on his life on March 30. Nancy was having a hard time deciding if she should go to the July 29 wedding alone. The president kept encouraging her because he felt it would be good for her after the stress and sadness of the past few months.

She finally decided, in the face of the urging of the president and their friends, to attend. We who always traveled with her were, of course, thrilled with the decision for our own selfish reasons.

Nancy began organizing herself, her wardrobe, and gifts for her hosts. Her personal secretary was constantly dashing from her own office to the private residence with boxes upon boxes.

I dispatched our press advance people to London where they would spend the next few weeks organizing every detail of Nancy's visit. Our social secretary was hard at work with the American embassy in London helping make last-minute arrangements for the American dinner.

I flew with Nancy and her guests, arriving a week before the wedding.

For days in advance of the actual wedding, there were nonstop parties, a reception at Buckingham Palace, and a highly publicized polo match in which Prince Charles would compete while his nervous fiancée watched.

The polo match was first up. What a treat. The Queen drove herself to the match, because, as I recall, it was on her property. The British press made much of our multicar motorcade in comparison to the Queen's understated arrival. They were also fascinated by one of our female Secret Service officers who was repeatedly photographed while she stood guard. The headline the next day under her picture: "Gun Girl."

Lady Diana sat under a tented area. It was possible to walk directly in front of her, within a few feet. I did just that and can still see her, a little bit slumped in her chair, biting her fingernails. I remember thinking at the time that she looked every bit the nineteen-year-old teenager who had to be under an amazing amount of pressure.

With no knowledge of the finer points of polo, we Americans took in the scene with thundering horses riding up and down the field, often close enough to our seats to throw turf up into our boxes. I have no idea who won, but at least Prince Charles emerged without injury.

The first formal social event was a wonderful private dinner party. Its hosts, Henry and Drue Heinz, were well-known Americans and loyal Reagan supporters. Their estate was overlooking a lake and we received word from our advance people that the hosts planned to have Nancy arrive by water, carried across the lake on a small "swan" boat. We managed to kill that plan; she arrived by car. She wanted to keep a low profile but her hosts, naturally, wanted lots of attention given to the arrival of the First Lady. The press was behind every hedgerow, so to speak. They were not allowed inside, as was the custom when royalty was present. As a result, the American press was counting on me to give them some "color" or background on the event. I remember feeling a bit of panic during the cocktail hour when several beautiful British women were talking "at" me. I said "at" not "with" because I could not understand a word they were saying. I remember feeling like Dorothy Parker, who wrote that she always felt like she had a papoose on her back when she was talking to an Englishman. It took me about an hour to adjust to the accent well enough to understand them and to mentally file away several stories to satisfy the needs of the American press.

I will never forget the butler at that dinner party. Partly because he was the first private butler I had ever met in my life but also because when I asked him for directions to the ladies' room he replied, "Oh, no, madam. Ladies hold their water at the Heinz estate." He read the confusion on my face, broke into a big smile, and showed me the way. Turns out his previous employer was Bing Crosby and he was known far and wide for his comedic talents.

Ambassador and Mrs. John J. Louis held a wonderful dinner one night during the week before the wedding, at Winfield House, the ambassador's official residence. We arranged for the American press to get some good pictures of the First Lady and, hopefully, reward us with favorable coverage. I worked all afternoon, figuring out how best to escort photographers from one area to another. That night, I walked that route one last time, deep in thought. Someone had changed the furniture around and before I knew it I found myself in the men's room! A man was very much present and a strong ammonia-like scent enveloped the room. You have never seen anyone whip around and get out of a room more quickly than I did.

The one-hundred-person dinner guest list was impressive. Among those in attendance were Princess Grace of Monaco and Princess Alexandra, cousin of the Queen, Walter and Lee Annenberg, Lord and Lady Astor, Edgar Bergen, the famous ventriloquist, the Bloomingdales, Marc Bohan of the House of Dior, Lord and Lady Soames, Mr. Harold Evans and Tina Brown, Mr. and Mrs. Douglas Fairbanks, Dr. and Mrs. Armand Hammer, Mr. and Mrs. Henry Heinz, Mr. and Mrs. Joseph Lauder, Ambassador and Mrs. Charles Price, General and Mrs. Bernard Rogers, US Army Supreme Allied Commander, Europe, and Barbara Walters.

Nancy's table was the center of the social event. She was flanked by Ambassador Louis and the Duke of Norfolk. The remaining seven guests at the table were: Princess Grace, Lord Carrington, the Chief of Protocol, the Duke of Marlborough, Mrs. Bloomingdale, Lord Soames, and Princess Alexandra. I remember watching the dinner from my vantage point and noticing that Nancy finally seemed to relax and enjoy herself after months of stress. Maybe the trip was working its magic.

Like the millions of viewers across the world, I watched the historic wedding itself on television. Several of us sat in comfort at the American ambassador's residence and watched it thanks to our wonderful hostess, Jo Louis.

Nancy represented our country well and we brought home some indelible memories. Nancy wore a soft peach ensemble by James Galanos with a silk crepe faille blouse, skirt, and coat embellished with a moiré lapel and a matching chiffon scarf and hat. Now, that was a mouthful. (It took a lot of skilled research to uncover the proper way to describe her outfit.)

I can still see Diana's dress and that huge train. Her engagement ring was so distinctive, a blue sapphire surrounded by diamonds. I raced to Harrods Department Store in London to buy replicas ($20.00 each) to take back to the States. Nancy's pal, Betsy Bloomingdale, was on our return flight and when she saw my fake she had to have it, so I gave one to her. I just wish I knew where mine is today. Lost to history or turning green on somebody else's finger.

* * *

Back in the good old USA, reality hit again. Altogether, the focus on decor, new china, and loaned clothing, added to the mingling with royalty, was creating an unfortunate—and to my mind inaccurate—early image of Nancy Reagan. Worse, it was against the backdrop of tough economic times. Nancy appeared to the public as insensitive and even selfish. We had been much too slow in getting on top of these issues.

Nancy recognized her image was at the point where it might begin to hurt the president, the last thing in the world she wanted to have happen. It was also high time the American public got a more fulsome view of the interests and concerns of the First Lady. And a better sense of her heart. The intense work to organize an effective campaign against youth drug abuse was finally under way. It would be another three months before we could launch.

4

Always an Actress

After a tough first year with lots of negative press coverage of the redecoration of the White House, revelations of borrowed designer gowns and jewelry, and a new Reagan china service, Nancy needed to work on her image. She knew it and was willing to help fix it.

The Gridiron Club, a Washington institution with a long, interesting history, would play a pivotal role in that process. The club was all male, made up of sixty members drawn from self-described elite Washington political reporters, from its inception in 1885. Ninety years later Helen Thomas organized a campaign to get women reporters included. The Gridiron comes together once a year to "roast" politicians based on the foibles of the past year—that is the club's sole reason for existence.

The Gridiron's traditions have been unchanged over the years. The white-tie audience is composed of mostly media elite sprinkled with well-known political figures. The evening always begins with the "Speech in the Dark" given by the club president. There are always red roses on the tables and a huge, eerie "Gridiron"-shaped light behind the head table. The roast performance is always a musical production, claiming to "singe but never burn." There is always a toast to the president and the evening ends with everyone standing and singing "Auld Lang Syne."

The Gridiron has another tradition, one that it ignores regularly. The dinner is "off the record," meaning no cameras, no recording, and no reporting of what happened that night. And yet, as soon as the evening ends, reporters report and major stories are prepared for Monday morning newspapers.

Over the years, I'd read those accounts of the Gridiron Dinner, always colorfully reported. Public figures who made "mistakes" during the preceding year typically were targeted for musical mockery.

I was fairly certain Nancy would be too juicy a target to pass up so I started talking to staffers about a month in advance. I talked with Mike Deaver and Jim Baker, to line up their support for my idea to have Nancy make a surprise appearance at the dinner. I knew she would want their opinion so I worked to stack the deck. Both agreed. Then I took the idea to Nancy who instantly liked the plan and gave me the green light to broach the subject with the Gridiron. I called Helen Thomas, dean of the White House Press Corps and an active member of the Gridiron, and asked her to feel out the club leadership as to their receptivity. Within an hour the president of the club was sitting in my office assuring me they would love her participation.

In the annals of Gridiron history, President Nixon and Vice President Agnew played a piano duet based on the infamous Nixon "southern strategy." In 1976 Betty Ford wowed the audience with a soft shoe dance. And one year the Carters did a jitterbug.

The club president explained to me that my suspicions were right. The club had already assembled the "Nancy" chorus of journalist singers who were rehearsing a version of "Second Hand Clothes" based on the song "Second Hand Rose," mocking her practice of wearing clothes furnished by well-known fashion designers like Adolfo, Galanos, Ralph Lauren, and Bill Blass.

Recently, I was amazed to find the yellowed typewritten lyrics that were furnished to me by my "mole" at the Gridiron. They'd been in my basement filing cabinet for thirty-six years. It was the song the reporters were going to sing mocking Nancy. My source thought it would help us respond, but just in case it didn't, they also furnished me with their suggestions for Nancy's musical response.

Here is what the Gridiron singers would open with: "Second Hand Clothes" based on the music of "Second Hand Rose" sung often slightly off-key:

I gave my second-hand clothes
To museum collections and traveling shows.
They were oh, so happy that they got 'em.
Won't notice they were ragged at the bottom.
Second-hand dress,
Good bye, you old worn out mess.

I never wear a frock more than just once.
Calvin Klein, Adolfo, Ralph Lauren and Bill Blass,
Ronald Reagan's mama's going strictly first class.
Rodeo Drive, I sure miss Rodeo Drive
In frumpy Washington.
Second-hand rings,
Donate those old used-up things.
Designers deduct 'em
We've living like kings.
So what if Ronnie's cutting back on welfare
I'll still wear a tiara in my coiffed hair.
Second-hand frock,
Press critics are such a crock,
Why don't they just hush up and go away.
Calvin Klein, Adolfo, Ralph Lauren and Bill Blass
Ronald Reagan's mama's going strictly first class
Rodeo Drive, I'll be back, Rodeo Drive
In nineteen eighty-five.

That closing line was to indicate Ronald Reagan would be a one-term president and the press was quietly pointing the finger at Nancy Reagan for being responsible. Singe, not burn?

The Gridiron Club recommended the following guidance for Nancy's entrance:

"As applause for the Gridiron song starts, a 7th Avenue garment rack is rolled out by a couple of bellboys. The clothes part and out comes Mrs. Reagan. She says:

'Hold it, hold it, hold it.
Colonel, could I see the score please?'

Mrs. R. looks through the score, tapping her foot.
'I have a few corrections. Hit it, Colonel.' (And then she begins
to sing.)
'Donnie Radcliffe, Helen Thomas and Judy Mann
Ronald Reagan's mama will now take a stand
Second hand news, you're peddling second hand news
The same old Washington blues.' "

With that they suggest Mrs. Reagan blow the audience a kiss and walk off arm in arm with the bellboys.

The Gridiron was suggesting that Nancy walk out and give them the back of her hand. As soon as I read this, I knew we were going to take an entirely different tack but we never told the Gridiron in advance. Nancy needed to make fun of herself, not blame the press.

With that knowledge, Landon Parvin, our talented speech-writer, went to work and wrote Nancy's response, also based on "Second Hand Rose":

I'm wearing second hand clothes,
Second hand clothes,
They're quite the style
In Spring fashion shows.
Even my new trench coat with fur collar,
Ronnie bought for ten cents on the dollar.
Second hand gowns,
And old hand-me-downs,
The china is the only thing that's new.
Even though they tell me that I'm no longer queen,
Did Ronnie have to buy me that new sewing machine?

Second hand clothes,
I'm wearing second hand clothes,
I sure hope Ed Meese sews.

I think my main contribution was to suggest "I sure hope Ed Meese sews" to the last line.

Instead of thumbing her nose at the press at the Gridiron, Nancy revealed her sense of humor and her willingness to take a chance to win back the media's goodwill by poking fun at herself, something of which they did not think she was capable. And the First Lady as songstress was a huge first for the Gridiron.

Nancy began to secretly rehearse her version of "Second Hand Clothes" well in advance while her staff, led by our intrepid social secretary, Muffie Brandon, created an outrageous outfit of mismatched and ill-fitting clothes, a hat, and rubber boots.

The morning of the big event the clothing was spirited away to the Capital Hilton in advance so that Nancy could surprise her husband with her unexpected appearance. In keeping with long-standing tradition, both the president and First Lady would be present, along with other members of the cabinet and senior staffers. It was important to Nancy to keep her appearance a secret from the president because that gave her the ability to focus on surprising him and not get nervous, she explained. That, as well as her experience as a movie actress many years earlier.

Landon remembers that she was still nervous and several times during the dinner asked him to sneak backstage and check that everything was in order. At one point he really needed to avail himself of the men's room. He raced inside, finding every urinal in use, so he ran into one of the stalls. Having never worn white tie and tails before, he forgot about the "tails" and as a result had white tie and wet tails the rest of the evening.

But I digress. Back to the stage.

The journalist/chorus sang its parody about Fancy Nancy without any knowledge that she was planning an appearance. In the middle of their song, Nancy left the head table with the audience assuming she was unhappy. Very unhappy. She'd told the president she needed to go to the ladies' room. The publisher sitting on my left, having taken note of her departure, leaned behind me and whispered to the publisher on my right, "Nancy Reagan just left. I bet she's pissed!" I pretended not to hear him. Meanwhile, my blood pressure was so high my head was pounding.

Moments later, having quickly changed into her costume, Nancy emerged from behind a rolling rack of clothes and began to sing. It took the audience at least thirty seconds to realize it was the First Lady dressed as the Bag Lady. The room felt electric. I turned to look at President Reagan and saw the real surprise in his eyes. He just lit up.

She was masterful. She'd taken her acting experience of thirty years previous to a new level, adding the ability to belt out a great song for her audience.

As she finished, she held up a fake piece of the new Reagan china and slammed it to the stage floor. It bounced across the floor but did not break.

The reporters and publishers, the broadcasters and producers had risen as one screaming their approval and demanded an encore. She obliged. At the end of her reprise, she once again slammed the plate to the floor and it smashed to smithereens. The response was even more enthusiastic.

Believe it or not, during those ten minutes of her performance, that Saturday night, the attitude in that room toward Nancy actually changed. You could feel it. She had them in the palm of her hand. The press was going to give her another chance and she was going to take full advantage of it.

It took real guts for Nancy to expose herself to the potential ridicule that a performance like this might generate. Nancy knew that. That's why she spent so much time on every detail of the lyrics, her outfit, and even her grand entrance. She deserved an Academy Award! And I think that if Ronald Reagan had been responsible for deciding who won the Academy Awards that year, she would have been a cinch for Best Actress.

As I mentioned, the Gridiron Dinner is officially off the record. However, reporters pay only lip service to that rule. I knew we were guaranteed to hear broadcasters' reports of Nancy's performance on Sunday and to see big news stories on Monday morning.

I was under orders not to brief any media with details in advance, but I felt duty bound to make sure one White House reporter did know about the Gridiron plan. Tom DeFrank worked for *Newsweek* and was writing a major cover story about Nancy with which we had cooperated. It was going to be on the newsstands across the country on Monday. *Newsweek* normally went to the printer on Friday night in order to hit the newsstands on Monday; the Gridiron Dinner was Saturday night. If I hadn't briefed *Newsweek* in advance, there was no way the reporter could include Nancy's surprise appearance. Even then, *Newsweek* had to hold back on printing that edition until after her triumphant Saturday night performance to be sure its report was accurate. To have no mention of Nancy's boffo appearance in its cover story would have been a major embarrassment for Tom and for *Newsweek*. I heard later that Tom DeFrank went to Mike Deaver to tell him the backstory and to make sure there would be no retribution for my decision. After it was all over and Nancy was basking in the novelty of glowing press accounts, I told her about the tensions behind the scenes. She simply rolled her eyes and told me not to give it a second thought.

And one of my most prized possessions is a White House picture of Nancy in her Gridiron wardrobe inscribed to me: "From your best dressed First Lady, Fondly, Nancy."

* * *

Nancy's early experiences onstage were invaluable on a number of occasions during the Reagan years. For instance, one of the most popular prime-time sitcoms on television in the early '80s was *Diff'rent Strokes*, featuring the young star Gary Coleman. The producer got in touch with us in 1982 and offered to involve Nancy in a drug education–themed program. Nancy sent me out to Hollywood ahead of her arrival to work with the writers on a script. I worked for several full days with the writers; we sat in a cottage on studio grounds as the story came to life. I faxed it back to the White House for comments; she reviewed it and made changes as well.

When Nancy got to Universal Studios, we spent an entire day on the set rehearsing and taping the show. She was a real pro. The producer had cue cards at the ready as the entire cast, including Nancy, began run-throughs of the show. She hardly needed those cue cards. The rehearsal and the taping went smoothly from start to finish.

The series was about two young African American brothers from Harlem taken in by a rich white widower. In this episode, Coleman's character, "Arnold," the younger brother, makes himself into an investigative reporter who finds out drugs are being sold at his elementary school. Arnold goes to the local newspaper with the story after he confirmed that one of the drug peddlers was selling "uppers, downers and goofballs." Nancy Reagan, playing herself, happens to be in New York the day the story broke in the newspaper. After reading about it, she goes to Arnold's home to learn the details and then goes to his school to warn the children about how dangerous these drugs are.

It was the first time any First Lady had ever actually played a substantive role in a television show and it got great ratings. This episode aired in 1983 to a very large audience, reaching millions of young people and their parents as well. By then her Just Say No campaign was in full swing and the appearance was key to introducing the initiative to the public.

* * *

On September 14, 1982, Grace Kelly, Princess Grace of Monaco, died in a tragic car crash. Nancy went to the funeral and stayed in Grace's apartment at the palace. I also went to the moving funeral, sitting way in the back. Then I waited for

Nancy while she attended the postfuneral reception hosted by Prince Rainier on the palace lawn. It was directly behind the princess's private apartment where my deputy, Barbara Cook Fabiani, and I waited. We were able to watch through louvered shutters on the windows and see Nancy as well as Princess Diana and others. Barbara and I were fascinated by a chaise lounge in the bedroom, which had a plaque attached noting that it was the birthing bed upon which Princess Grace delivered her babies.

Then, in March 1983, Nancy Reagan's acting background came in handy once again when she was asked to fill in for Princess Grace. Before her death, Princess Grace had agreed to come to Washington to narrate "Carnival of the Animals," a "grand zoological fantasy" according to its composer Camille Saint-Saëns. The occasion was a special Kennedy Center performance by the National Symphony to benefit the Musicians Pension Fund. The celebrated Mstislav Rostropovich, a world-famous Russian cellist, would conduct.

Leonard Silverstein, who over the years has chaired the National Symphony, the White House Historical Society, the National Gallery of Art among others, and his equally accomplished wife, Elaine, came up with the idea of asking the First Lady to take the stage in place of Princess Grace.

Nancy was pleased to accept and proud to fill in for Princess Grace. "I said yes because Grace was my friend," said Nancy.

To prepare, Nancy rehearsed with Rostropovich, fondly known as "Slava," concentrating on Ogden Nash's tongue-twisting words like "tortley, turtley, torpor." And "pterodactyls and brontosauruses."

Slava brought his dog Pooks along to one of the rehearsals

at the White House, according to the *New York Times.* On command in Russian, the dog jumped on the piano bench and began to paw the ivories. That had to be a first in the history of musical moments in the White House.

Princess Caroline and Prince Albert joined President Reagan in the presidential box for the bittersweet performance that evening.

Nancy admitted to a case of nerves at the beginning of her performance before a packed house, but said she had a strong sense that Grace was looking down on her and that feeling helped calm her.

Knowing Nancy as I did, I am quite certain that when she left us a few years ago she immediately went in search of Grace to make sure her performance passed muster.

5

Just Say No

Nancy also deserves a great deal of credit for the impact she
had on young people in the '80s with her Just Say No campaign
against drugs.

—George H.W. Bush, April 20, 2017

Within days of the 1981 inauguration, Nancy's staff, following her direction, began organizing a series of educational
meetings for Nancy and her senior staff with all the interest
groups surrounding the drug prevention and treatment issues
at the time. The staff was not at all certain that this tough issue—a downer in our minds—was the best project for Nancy
to adopt. Nancy finally put us straight. She said, "If I am going
to be involved in an issue for four or even eight years, it has to
be something I really care about. I care about what drugs are
doing to our young people." Case closed.

Fearless leader and project director Ann Wrobleski was in
perfect sync with Nancy. She became an expert on every interest group and every aspect of the drug problem. Ann was at
the table when the president's new drug czar began to develop
administration policy on the issue. She knew that if the First
Lady was to lead an effective campaign, it needed to align
with the president's policies and it needed to survive beyond
his presidency, independent of federal funding.

By the fall of 1981, we were ready to begin a public rollout of the campaign and Nancy was eager to get started. We hit the road, crisscrossing the country, drawing attention to the depth of the drug epidemic destroying our young people. And because of Nancy's focus and hard work over the next seven years, countless lives were saved.

We started the campaign by traveling to visit Phoenix House, Straight, Inc., and other treatment centers around the country, where recovering addicts told Nancy their stories and listened to her talk about her personal pride in their recovery.

Everywhere we went—Dallas, Little Rock, Tampa to name a few—we took press with us. Early on the press was skeptical, figuring this was a PR initiative meant for photo ops with no real commitment. But by the end of the first year of travel and hard work, those reporters recognized Nancy's real commitment to the drug abuse issue and began to take her seriously.

Nancy wanted to help change youth public opinion on drug use; her goal was to push back against the "normalization" of the use of marijuana and other harmful drugs. She admired the campaign against tobacco that had convinced children to carry the antitobacco message home and pressure their parents to quit smoking. She believed instilling strong negative feelings about drugs in children at an early age would provide benefits to those children, and society, in the long run.

By late 1982 the press skepticism had gradually turned to measured admiration as they traveled with us across the country and witnessed her commitment, her focus, and the emotional way young people responded to her.

In her travels Nancy related most closely to the organically formed "parent groups" that functioned as local activists. These groups grew out of the rapidly increasing recognition that most parents were clueless about the rampant drug use among young people and, when faced with a drug-dependent child, had no idea how to get help. The parent groups were the first line of defense: they educated parents and provided support for shell-shocked parents in need of direction.

The parent groups became a vital and valuable resource for those families dealing with drug abuse. When Nancy started working with them, they were loosely organized as a countrywide federation called Parents Resource Institute for Drug Education, or PRIDE. The PRIDE organization was run primarily out of Georgia Southern University in Atlanta by a PhD named Buddy Gleason. Others, including Bill and Pat Barton and Joyce Nalepka, had helped form the National Federation of Parents for Drug-Free Youth. They began to lobby Congress and state legislatures for appropriate regulatory action and fiscal support for treatment.

The work of the parent groups was bolstered considerably by a multimillion-dollar donation from a Gulf State prince and sent to the First Lady (which, I hasten to add, was legal at the time) and that Nancy immediately forwarded to the parent groups to make sure their work was sustainable into the future. In fact, the successor organization of the National Federation of Parents for Drug-Free Youth—the National Family Partnership—is alive and well today. And, sadly, needed more than ever.

I vividly remember one early trip to Dallas where Nancy met with parents who were dealing with drug problems involving their own children. For them, her interest was a lifeline and their gratitude for her visit was palpable. What I remember most clearly from that meeting was how closely Nancy listened to them. The meeting was private; no reporters were present. I remember thinking that Nancy was going to surprise a lot of people when the press realized they had greatly underestimated Nancy's resolve. And her effectiveness.

Nancy traveled thousands of miles in the United States to visit young people in treatment and give them the encouragement that comes from being praised by a First Lady. She never seemed tired. The progress she was making seemed to energize her. Even when her staff was exhausted, she never stopped moving forward.

One visit to a treatment program had a funny behind-the-scenes situation that we never forgot. At a summer camp in Arkansas, one of the young boys was chosen to present Nancy with a gift. Fortunately, the advance team of Bob Gubitosi and Barbara Cook Fabiani noticed an inked tattoo on the back of his hand. That hand would be highly visible to the TV cameras and reporters who were traveling with us. Bob grabbed his own pen and changed the "F" of a certain four-letter word to a "B." Ever after that, we always referred to the young boy as Buck. And I sincerely hope he is well and thriving.

One day at the White House, Nancy took a call from a hysterical mother in Texas who was desperate for help for her drug-addicted son. I listened in to that call. Nancy wrote down her name and number and promised the mother she would have someone get back to her with help. She got off that call and promptly called Robbie Robinson in Dallas who ran the Texas War on Drugs group funded by Ross Perot. Robbie promised to get help for the boy the next day and Nancy said, "No, Robbie, today, not tomorrow. This lady does not need to spend one more sleepless night worrying about whether her son will live until tomorrow." Needless to say, that young man was placed into treatment that very night. Nancy checked back with the family and at last report the young man was doing very well.

In our efforts to expand the Just Say No campaign beyond US borders, we borrowed a format used by President Nixon as part of his War on Drugs. He had brought twenty US ambassadors back to Washington to participate in a discussion of what more the United States could do globally to stop the spread of illegal drugs. His point was that the drug epidemic was a global problem and he wanted America's diplomats on the front line. In early 1985, we organized a similar meeting with thirty US ambassadors.

The White House Office of Drug Policy was closely involved in Nancy's Just Say No campaign and very supportive of the effort to take our program beyond our borders. Vice President George H.W. Bush was then responsible for coordinating all US government programs dealing with the enforcement of antidrug policy. He attended and spoke at the meeting as did the director of National Drug Control Policy, the attorney general, and other senior administration officials. Nancy had no trouble lining up the top talent!

The ambassadors were complimentary of Nancy's campaign; several urged that she visit the countries to which they were accredited to draw attention to the problem and lend support to those leaders who were supportive of US efforts. After several months of sometimes heated discussion between White House, State Department, and Secret Service interests about the prospects for an overseas First Lady antidrug tour, the final answer was not no; it was NOT A CHANCE. The cocaine cartels were on the upswing and no one wanted to take responsibility for Nancy's safety. Nancy was disappointed but she had complete faith in the Secret Service and accepted the decision.

Instead, we decided to try to bring other countries to us. In April of 1985, eighteen First Ladies from around the world—from Pakistan to Colombia to Japan to Italy—joined Nancy for a meeting in the East Room of the White House followed by a trip to Atlanta to attend the annual PRIDE conference at Georgia State University. Security was tight, protocol was strict, logistics were complex. Each of the eighteen First Ladies had her own limo but they all had to share a plane to Atlanta and back. Those First Ladies seemed to develop a bond on that trip. They had a clear understanding that programs and strategies existed that were effective in beating back drug abuse, and they seemed energized by the conference. It was a long day but more than worth it. Drug awareness education made major news around the world that day.

Nancy was committed to her campaign for all her years in the White House. In late October 1988, as the Reagan administration was drawing to a close, Nancy became the first First Lady to address the General Assembly of the United Nations. Flanked by Secretary of State George Shultz and US Ambassador to the United Nations Vernon Walters, she spoke about the challenges of drug abuse and drug awareness. She also described the shared responsibilities among countries where drugs were grown, countries through which drugs were trafficked, and countries where drugs were consumed. She cast a wide net and called all within it to action. After her speech, the First Ladies who'd met at the White House three years earlier met again to discuss their progress. Secretary Shultz said he sensed a real resolve in these ladies.

* * *

Nancy Reagan showed herself to be very effective in using the power of the media to help save many young people from ever using drugs; she raised significant monies to help treatment and prevention programs, and to reach kids or kids in need. She helped educate First Ladies from across the globe about how to help change attitudes in their own countries.

She traveled across the country and ultimately the world working to educate kids to avoid drugs, to get treatment for those in need of it, and, perhaps every bit as significant, to raise awareness among parents of the peer pressure their children faced. I don't think I am overstating when I say Nancy Reagan led her staff to create a strong public education effort to shine powerful klieg lights on a dark corner of our country and across the world where young kids were introduced to dangerous drugs by their peers and sometimes even by their parents. Her impact over more than a decade was powerful and saved many young people of that generation from the ravages of drugs.

According to the White House Council on National Drug

Control Policy in 1979, almost 10 percent of eighteen- to twenty-five-year-olds reported using cocaine; eight years later—the Just Say No years—the number was reduced to less than 5 percent. Regarding marijuana, the twelve- to seventeen-year-olds had a dramatic drop during the same eight years from roughly 14 percent use down to 5.4 percent. And according to Gallup's Youth Survey, the percentage of teens admitting to marijuana use continued to drop from 38 percent in 1981 to 20 percent in 1989. Those numbers certainly bolster the case that it is possible to change minds and habits on the issue of drug use if we persist.

The daily barrage of news stories about the opioid epidemic in the United States is more than discouraging. We could sure use the help of another Nancy Reagan with the platform and the courage to convince today's young people to Just Say No.

6

Protector in Chief

March 1981. Spring was in the air. The Reagans were set-
tling into life at the White House and we were all beginning
to feel at home. The first state dinner had been beautifully
executed; we had started planning the Just Say No campaign.
I was busy planning media opportunities.

Then Nancy faced the biggest challenge of her married life
on March 30, 1981.

The First Lady was at a luncheon at the National Trust
for Historic Preservation in nearby Georgetown. Over dessert
Nancy caught my eye and indicated she was ready to leave. It
was shortly after 2:00 p.m. She said her goodbyes to Michael
Ainslie, the president of the National Trust. After a short drive
back to the White House, I headed toward my office while she
took the elevator to the private residence. My phone was ringing as I walked into my office. It was Jennefer Hirshberg, a
reporter for the *Washington Star*, telling me that they heard on
the police radio that shots had been fired outside the Capital

Hilton and wanted to know if I knew anything. I said no and immediately dropped the phone. I ran back down the hall toward the residence elevator. I wasn't thinking; I was operating out of pure instinct. Nancy Reagan came down the hall toward me, moving swiftly. That's when I knew she had heard the same news.

She had just learned that there had been a shooting from George Opfer, her lead Secret Service agent. At that point no one knew that the president himself had been shot. George recommended she stay in the safety of the residence until we had more information. Nancy was having none of that.

She simply said, "No, he needs me."

We raced to George Washington Hospital in about five minutes. Mike Deaver stood outside waiting for her. There we first learned that President Reagan had been shot by a deranged young man—a schizophrenic—who thought actress Jodie Foster would be attracted to him if he killed the president.

I think the First Lady went into shock. She became very quiet once they took the president into surgery. I was standing in the hallway leading into the operating room. They wheeled him past me (and what seemed like every doctor within a five-mile radius) and he saw Chief of Staff Jim Baker, White House Counselor Ed Meese, and Mike Deaver standing directly across from me, all three of them looking morose. President Reagan raised his head—I vividly remember seeing the muscles and tendons in his neck strain—and he said to them, "Who's minding the store?" All three broke out in big smiles of relief.

As I rode with Nancy on the elevator up to the hospital chapel we held hands. I kept saying, "It's going to be all right." She did not say a word. When we talked about it later, she did not remember me, the elevator, holding hands, or anything I said. She went into the chapel where Sarah Brady was praying for Jim. Jim Baker joined Nancy and they prayed together. He told me she was really shaken.

I recall feeling useless and searching for something to do. I started asking nurses to help me find out who else was injured and what hospital they were in. That's when one nurse told me that Jim Brady had died. That's what the media was reporting. I quickly found out that was not true and ran back to her to tell her not to repeat that because it really was not true. But living with the belief that Jim had died for just those few minutes before I learned the truth—that he was in fact alive and down the hall at GW hospital—was incredibly painful. And the next day, as I was leaving the hospital, Sarah Brady was standing in the hall outside Jim's room. She insisted I come in; I tried to say no, that I didn't want to disturb him. What I really didn't want was to see him. Sarah pushed me into the room, ahead of her, and said "Jim, look, Sheila Tate is here." He made some effort to say something—not intelligible, just a groan of recognition—and all I could do was look with horror at his bandaged head. It was more than double its normal size. I left that room and, for the first time since the shooting, I walked outside where I began to cry; I fully expected Jim to die before the night was over.

* * *

Nancy focused entirely on her husband's recovery. She spent every day at his bedside. She brought him something different every day, like Jelly Belly jelly beans, his favorite candy. She taped Get Well cards from across the nation and funny notes from children all over his walls. She invited him to dance as they walked down the halls to get him exercise. AP reporter Maureen Santini reported a particularly moving account of a telegram the president received from his old pal Jimmy Stewart saying, "I would have taken that bullet."

I talked to Nancy frequently in the immediate aftermath, usually at my instigation, to get any information that I could provide to the press. The day after his surgery, I was in the adjoining room at the hospital, helping Patti and Ron, two of their children, with statements they wanted to release to the media. Nancy said to me, "Can you hear that?" It was a slapping, pounding sound. She said the nurses were beating on the president's back to keep him from getting congested. I can still hear that sound if I stop and think about it. And I vividly remember how Nancy winced with every pounding.

Mr. Hinckley was unsuccessful in his bizarre plan to kill Ronald Reagan, but he wreaked havoc on the life of our wonderful, ebullient presidential press secretary, Jim Brady, who died in 2016. Jim took a bullet in the middle of his forehead. He was never truly Jim again; he was a shadow of his former self, confined to a wheelchair and fighting complications for the rest of his life until he succumbed to those injuries thirty-five years later. Hinckley murdered him; it just took thirty-five painful years for Jim to die. Jim will always be my hero.

There were many heroes on March 30, 1981.

President Reagan very likely would have died if his Secret

Service agent, Jerry Parr, had not thrown him into the limo. Jerry ordered the driver to head straight for the White House, but within a few minutes he spotted foamy red blood on the president's lips and realized the president had been injured and ordered the driver to proceed to nearby GW Hospital. At the time, even Jerry did not know the president had been shot; at first he assumed he'd broken the president's rib when he shoved him into the car and threw himself on top of President Reagan.

DC police officer Thomas K. Delahanty was shot in the neck; that bullet ricocheted off his spinal cord and created permanent nerve damage to his left arm. Officer Delahanty's injuries forced his retirement from a career he loved. The docs who operated to remove the Devastator bullet from his body had to wear bulletproof vests in case it exploded during the surgery.

Secret Service Agent Tim McCarthy put himself in the line of fire as he was trained to do. When he spread his body in front of President Reagan, he took a bullet to the abdomen. He recovered and subsequently became one of Nancy's agents before retiring. He eventually moved back to Illinois where he is still serving the public, now as police chief of a town in his home state. He was like every agent I knew in the Presidential Protective Detail, a mixture of courage, modesty, and decency.

* * *

Oddly, I think Ronald Reagan recovered more quickly than Nancy. After that day, March 30, 1981, she was a wreck whenever he left the safe confines of the White House, worrying about his safety.

Nancy had always been attentive to her husband's schedule because, as she told me, his staff tended to cram his day with one event after another from morning until evening with little or no time between meetings. She insisted that he did not function well with an overloaded schedule so she kept the pressure on to space out his meetings and give him breaks.

This was especially true when she was away from the White House. Once on a trip we were sitting in her hotel room at the Sands Hotel in Las Vegas (which was actually Frank Sinatra's private apartment), where she was scheduled to speak to the National PTA on the subject of youth drug abuse and prevention. The president's schedule for the next day came across a fax machine; she looked at it and handed it to me saying, "This is what I mean." His day was set to start at 8 a.m. and end at 11 p.m. She made a call and the schedule was moderated a bit. Quite a bit, as I recall.

Just as she always did when out of town, she also called her husband. As he came on the line, she settled back against the bed pillows, put her feet up on the bed, looked up, and burst out laughing. The ceiling above the bed was mirrored. She could hardly get the words out to tell the president because she was laughing so hard.

Nancy was frequently criticized by the press for always being on the phone. She called her mother every single evening just to tell her she loved her. If she and the president were not together, they called each other daily. Nancy kept in close touch with her lifelong friends by calling them. She'd quickly learned that they were reluctant to call her because they assumed she was busy. After I left her staff, I became one of the privileged who received frequent calls. But for some reason the press thought her affinity for keeping in telephonic touch was some kind of a personal defect.

I think her anxiety about Reagan's schedule gave rise to her secret dependence on astrology. She began conferring with a West Coast astrologer about "safe" days for the president to travel. I never knew about this practice until it became public, though I do know that Nancy never used astrology to determine her own schedule. Jim Baker told me he did not know about it for several years. Mike Deaver was the only one who knew and he kept it to himself. Nancy's "protective" astrological scheduling became public thanks to a book by former chief of staff Donald Regan and the media went wild. I had only recently left the White House when the book came out and "Katie bar the door" as my mother used to say. I went out to lunch that day, and when I walked back into my office, I had at least fifty phone messages from various reporters and media outlets awaiting me. It wasn't hard to figure something big had happened. So first I called the White House and asked Elaine Crispin, the new press secretary, what was going on. She told me about the astrology and said they thought it would be a one-day story. I could not have disagreed more. I told Elaine that unless they did something to diffuse it, this astrology business would be like an albatross around her neck. I really felt heartsick.

Looking back, Nancy's reliance on astrology just seems silly to me but at the time the revelation that the president's schedule was determined by an astrologer in California was very troubling and very damaging. However, understanding her anxiety about his safety, I can excuse her reliance on the astrologer. Sort of.

Their son, Ron, also inspired Nancy's protective insights. For his own reasons he decided to sign away his right to Secret Service protection. It's not unusual these days and generally goes unreported when adult children eschew armed guards, but at the time it was too juicy a story for someone not to leak it to the press.

When I told Nancy about the press inquiry from one of the New York tabloids about Ron's lack of security, she burst into tears. Her husband came immediately from the Oval Office after hearing about it. The president had just escaped a potentially lethal bullet wound even with Secret Service protection; now their son was without any protection whatsoever and it was about to become public knowledge. The parents were understandably beside themselves. Nancy was as upset as I ever saw her, inconsolable about the idea that Ron had left himself so vulnerable. After what they had been through, she had every right to be fearful. And I suspect the hardest part was that she was helpless to do anything to ensure his protection.

Much later I learned that Patti had also shed her Secret Service protection but luckily that never surfaced publicly during Reagan's presidency.

* * *

President Reagan actually forgave Hinckley. He was quoted as telling the Pope that he realized that as a Christian he had a duty to forgive him. I don't believe Nancy ever did. I took some comfort in the fact that Nancy had died before Hinckley was set free to live in Williamsburg, Virginia, under the supervision of his mother, who is over ninety years old.

I read that Officer Delahanty was not "enthused" to learn that Hinckley was being released from the mental hospital, St. Elizabeths, in DC, in 2016.

Many Americans did not know that for the remainder of President Reagan's terms, Jim Brady retained the title of press secretary to the president; he also retained his salary and benefits, at the president's insistence. While Jim was never able to actually resume his duties, he was included in everything as much as possible.

I still smile when I remember one encounter between the Reagans several months after the shooting. The president had just been given medical clearance to go back to work part-time in the Oval Office. She and I were going somewhere. We were in the downstairs "cross hall" about to walk out the door to get into her limo. The president came running down the hall toward her; he wanted to say goodbye to her before she left. She saw him running and her protective instincts kicked in; she instantly put up her hands, telling him to slow down. He said with a big smile on his face, "I can't help it. It's my boyish exuberance!"

7

The Perfectionist

I have often wondered why the term "perfectionist" is an implied criticism. People often asked me if it wasn't hard working for a perfectionist like Nancy. I readily describe Nancy Reagan as a perfectionist. I consider it a compliment. And I enjoyed working for someone who knew what she wanted.

Nancy was a perfectionist when it came to her home, and since her home was going to be the White House, she was eager to get that house in order, so to speak. She was naturally a "nester" and she wanted to get settled before she went to the next item on her comprehensive checklist. She also wanted, I think, to weave a cocoon of comfort and stability around her family's lives.

Quite logically, Nancy's attention to detail also extended to entertaining. She worked with the same thoroughness on everything. My records indicate there were fifty-six official state dinners during the Reagan administration and several reciprocal dinners overseas. When I left in February 1985, I had handled press for thirty-two of them. I was sad to read how seldom the Clintons or President Bush 43 hosted state dinners. Truly, missed opportunities. They were such elegant events and often helped improve understanding and cement relations between the United States and the guest countries. Nancy felt they were very important and she really worked to make sure every detail of every dinner was considered. I doubt any administration since has held as many state dinners as the Reagans or, for that matter, made as many diplomatic friends.

Muffie Brandon was Nancy's first social secretary and is a great friend to me. She worked closely with Nancy to establish an incredibly detailed checklist for state dinners that was used to organize each of them during the eight years of the Reagan administration. Muffie says Nancy was deeply interested and involved in the planning of every dinner. If you have ever orchestrated a daughter's wedding, you know how complicated it becomes. Now imagine organizing a far more complicated state dinner every month for eight years. The only significant gap in that schedule was due to the March 30, 1981, assassination attempt.

Here's how they typically came together.

The National Security Council or the State Department would notify Chief of Staff Jim Baker or Deputy Chief of Staff Mike Deaver of a pending state visit that would include a formal state dinner. From that point, Nancy and Muffie took over.

The State Department would send Muffie a suggested guest list, often including distinguished Americans whose family originated in the country of the visiting head of state.

Nancy got deeply involved in the guest list and would go

over suggested names with Muffie. She would add names and delete others. As Muffie said, "We developed an unofficial quota system with set numbers of guests from the Senate, the House of Representatives, the American ambassador to the guest country as well as the current ambassador from the visiting country to the United States. Vice President and Mrs. Bush were always included."

We also had a set number of senior White House staff and several reporters or publishers with their spouses. Jim Brady and I selected the media guests. After Jim was shot two months after the inauguration, Larry Speakes and I made the recommendations.

Nancy and Muffie reviewed lists of distinguished Americans, often with ties to the visiting country; they came from the arts, education, science, and medicine. Personal friends of the Reagans were also often included, usually members of Governor Reagan's famous kitchen cabinet.

Muffie and Nancy would discuss the menu with the head chef and make certain that there were no dietary restrictions or special religious observances to honor. Menus reflected the best in American cuisine. And California wines, of course, were favored.

These dinners were an important extension of the diplomatic outreach by the Reagan administration. Nancy was intent on making certain their guests felt honored by the evening's events. Nancy would personally choose the decor, the color of the table coverings, the china, and the flowers. She frequently had advance tastings of the menu and a preview of the proposed floral arrangements.

As you can imagine, an invitation to a Reagan state dinner was highly coveted; Muffie regularly received desperate requests for help getting invited. Nancy decided from the beginning that the guest lists were to be limited to 120 people for every State Dining Room dinner. No exceptions. The 120-person limit was established principally to allow room for our waiters to move easily between tables, but it also added an aura of exclusivity that a state dinner deserves.

To accommodate the larger visiting party, typically thirty people, not invited to the dinner, Nancy and Muffie established an alternative dinner held in the downstairs garden room and hosted by senior White House staffers. That "alternative" group always joined the state dinner guests for the evening entertainment in the East Room.

Seating, as you can imagine, was incredibly sensitive. Nancy was very attentive to it. Explained Muffie: "She and I would sit down, often in the calligrapher's office with the names of each guest on pink or blue slips of paper, laying out a seating plan for each table of eight. Nancy was very detail oriented and especially attentive to the president's table. She was more concerned with personal dynamics than protocol. Sometimes it took a call with Chief of Protocol Leonore Annenberg to settle protocol issues. When we finished this exercise, I would type up the agreed-upon seating arrangements and send it up to her. Corrections, reassignments, revisions were often made until we got final approval from Nancy. Then, and only then, would the calligraphers go to work creating the seating cards and menus."

Nancy and the president often reminded Muffie that they

wanted these dinners to be fun as well as memorable. They wanted an atmosphere of relaxed glamor where people could get to know one another a bit before more serious meetings began the next day. They wanted their guests and friends to feel the warmth of their hospitality.

One of the best-kept secrets was the role of Frank Sinatra in the selection of the entertainment for these state dinners. Muffie said, "I would propose names of singers, opera stars, musicians, ballet dancers and if 'Old Blue Eyes' objected to my recommendations, he would come up with an alternative."

Added to all the complexities of planning was the presence of photographers and reporters who captured and opined on every detail. This is where I came in, along with my hard-working assistants, Barbara Cook Fabiani and Betsy Koons Robertson. At the beginning of the evening we escorted photographers to the North Portico to cover the arrival of our honored guests. Then I picked them up again in the press office and took them to cover the foursome as they descended the grand staircase to the State Floor at the conclusion of a short visit in the private residence. As guests arrived downstairs at the Diplomatic Reception Room, they had to walk a gauntlet of photographers and reporters asking questions and taking pictures.

We had several "reporters" who held very old credentials and didn't actually write for anyone. They were always there to cover a state dinner. I used to enjoy watching guests like Henry Kissinger or Douglas Fairbanks stop to answer questions from the faux reporters, completely unaware of whom they were talking to.

After the actual state dinner began, we working staffers had a quick dinner in the White House mess with the White House doctor and several other aides who were required to be in the building. Next, we ushered photographers into the State Dining Room with their stepladders to photograph the president's toast. During a short social hour after dinner, I took several social reporters to the State Floor where they could mingle with guests for a few minutes and get some quotes for their stories. Next, all the press were moved into the East Room where they watched and photographed the entertainment from risers.

The event was not exactly relaxing for the First Lady's East Wing press operation. But the media with whom we worked were usually seasoned White House reporters; the photographers knew where they needed to be and the social press were usually well behaved as well. Not that we didn't have a few confrontations. The Reagans did not want the reporters who mingled with guests to use tape recorders; I took a lot of heat for that decision. The reporters argued that they used tape recorders to make sure they reported guest remarks accurately. Sometimes I thought it was because they got lazy and didn't want to take careful notes. Occasionally some photographers got elbowed out of a good photo opportunity by a photographer from the guest country. I got good at giving them both the eagle eye. The diplomatic eagle eye.

It's great fun now to think of the celebrity guests at one state dinner or another over the years, people like Richard Chamberlain, Douglas Fairbanks, Claudette Colbert, Efrem Zimbalist Jr., Art Linkletter, Ann Landers, Dinah Shore, Lee

Trevino, Jacques Cousteau, Benny Goodman, Rock Hudson, Frank Sinatra, Perry Como, Charlton Heston, Rhonda Fleming, Mary Martin, Dina Merrill, Debbie Reynolds, John Updike, Edgar Bergen, and Andy Warhol just to name a few. But it was hard work at the time.

Nancy told me she wanted every person who attended an event in the Reagan White House to remember it as the highlight of his or her life. A few years after leaving the White House, I returned as a guest for the state dinner for President Mubarak. It was a glorious evening. I truly loved knowing that was why the First Lady worked so hard to make sure each event was special. Or, in other words, perfect.

* * *

Funerals are always time for reflection. When Nancy died in 2016, many of us attended her memorial service at the Reagan Library and started reminiscing, telling stories, laughing and crying.

We all agreed on one thing: her funeral was perfect. Of course it was. She had planned it. That is what a perfectionist does.

Even the weather acceded to her wishes. She did not like rain. The winds picked up during the service, but the rains held off until it was over. Then, the skies opened up.

Just as the rain began to pour, she was reunited with her greatly loved husband in the tomb on the Reagan Library grounds looking west to the mountains.

I leave it to the reader to decide if being a perfectionist is a bad thing. I suspect you know my conclusion.

8

Family Ties

All happy families are alike; each unhappy family is unhappy in its own way.

—From *Anna Karenina* by Leo Tolstoy

When Nancy Reagan came into this world, she was named Anne Frances Robbins. Born in Queens, New York, on July 6, 1921, she had no silver spoon in her mouth.

Her mother, Edith Luckett Robbins, was born in 1888 and was a native of Petersburg, Virginia. She was the youngest of nine children. Edith (Edie) Luckett's family moved to Washington, DC, but the story goes that for each of the nine births her mother returned to Petersburg because she didn't want her children to be "damn Yankees."

Nancy Reagan's father, Kenneth Seymour Robbins, came from a prosperous New Jersey family and was educated at Princeton. Apparently, what he lacked was ambition. He was working as a car salesman when he met his future wife.

Edie had enough ambition for both of them. She quit school at age sixteen to pursue an acting career, performing up and down the East Coast with a number of well-known actors— Walter Huston, Spencer Tracy, and the silent film star named Alla Nazimova who would in time become Nancy's godmother.

Edie and Ken married in 1916 and eventually moved to New York so Edie could pursue her career. Ken became an insurance salesman. In 1917, when the United States entered the war, Ken enlisted. He returned two years later, and two years after that Nancy was born.

The couple separated in 1922. Ken moved to New Jersey to live with his mother; Edie took over full responsibility for the baby. She refused alimony, believing she could support herself and her child on her own. Nancy went everywhere with her for the first two years. When it became impossible to care for Nancy alone and continue to pursue her career, Edie arranged to leave Nancy with her sister and her husband, Virginia and C. Audley Galbraith, in Bethesda, Maryland.

When she was age-eligible, Nancy and her cousin, Charlotte, three years her senior, attended the Sidwell Friends School together in Washington, DC. Whenever Edie visited, which she did regularly, she'd teach Nancy and Charlotte the latest dance craze. Nancy caught the acting bug.

Edie met neurosurgeon Loyal Davis in 1927 when both were sailing to Europe on the SS *New York*. Before Loyal and Edie married in 1929, when Nancy was eight, Edie insisted on getting Nancy's permission. The answer, you may safely assume, was yes. Nancy moved to Chicago to live with the newlyweds and eventually attended Girls Latin School there. Loyal's son from his first marriage—Richard—remained, at first, with his mother in Beverly Hills.

Speaking of Girls Latin, I have a copy of the letter dated May 4, 1982, that Nancy sent to Mrs. Peterson's third-grade class who had invited her to visit and have lunch. She asked the boys and girls to save her a seat in the lunchroom on May 14. I vividly remember Nancy sitting in that cafeteria surrounded by third graders and having a wonderful time. It was as if she was transported back to her happy childhood memories when Girls Latin played a big role in her life.

Nancy's biological father gave her up for adoption when Nancy asked him to. She'd seen Kenneth Robbins only sporadically for many years. By then she thought of Loyal Davis as her father. She bristled when, during the White House years, reporters referred to him as her stepfather. And, at the same time, she never uttered a negative word about Kenneth Robbins as long as I knew her.

Anne Frances Robbins—called Nancy from birth—was adopted by Loyal Davis and officially became Nancy Davis.

And it stands to reason that she would adore the man who brought her the first taste of permanent family stability when she was eight years old and allowed her to spend the rest of her youth with two devoted parents and a younger brother.

I spent some time talking with Nancy's little brother, Dr. Richard A. Davis, to explore those early years. Dick was four years old and Nancy was eight when his father and her mother married and they became a family. Though he lived with his mother, he would spend summers and holidays in Chicago with his dad, Edie, and Nancy. When his mother died from TB while he was still quite young, he moved to Chicago to join his father's family. Dick said that from the very beginning Nancy was thoughtful and kind to him. She even used to take him with her on her dates.

Dick Davis spent his adult years as a neurosurgeon, just

like his dad. He trained at Northwestern and practiced at the University of Pennsylvania in the Philadelphia area. He and his wife, Pat, were always close to Nancy.

His first memory of Nancy is playing their favorite game together: it was called "Help, Murder, Police." Thinking I had misheard him, I asked Dr. Davis to repeat the name of the game. I hadn't misheard. So then I asked him what the rules of the game were. He laughed and said, "It mainly involved jumping on the furniture." It makes me laugh just thinking of Nancy jumping on the couch, yelling "Help! Murder! Police!"

* * *

I believe that to understand the unique dynamics of a family you must be one of its members. And even then, family members may have differing memories of the same event.

The media portrayed the Reagan family as peculiar, with the children frozen out of the exclusive husband/wife nucleus. To some degree, the children reinforced that image. Maureen Reagan was the eldest, the daughter of Ronald Reagan and actress Jane Wyman. Michael Reagan was her brother, adopted by Ronald Reagan and Jane Wyman. The president and Nancy had two children, Patti and Ron. Even at Nancy's funeral, Patti in her moving, sad, and funny eulogy referred to her parents as "two halves of a circle, closed tight around a world in which their love for each other was the only sustenance they needed."

Early in the first term, Nancy asked me to spend a day with her at her California home where she was packing the last of their belongings for storage or transfer to the White House.

I jumped at the chance to see material I might use to help acquaint the American public with the Reagans.

Nancy had drawers in the master bedroom overflowing with pictures of the family: it seemed like each child's birthday party was photographed or videotaped; there were photos of Ronald Reagan tossing children in the air in the middle of the family swimming pool. Nancy spent hours with me, sitting on the bedroom floor, reminiscing about each event with genuine fondness and love in her voice.

There were wonderful photos of the entire family including Maureen and Mike.

As an outsider, I became skeptical of the media description of the family. In their rush to judgment they seemed to draw the worst possible explanation for any and every event in the Reagan family life.

From my personal observations, Nancy Reagan was very family oriented. Her devotion to her mother knew no bounds. As I mentioned earlier, she called her every single evening, just to check in and say she loved her. I stood with her in the White House residence living room where she held a photo album close to her chest, stroking it while she told me about her father, Loyal Davis, who had recently died. She spoke through tears about how much he enhanced her life. As a youngster, she loved going with him to the hospital and watching from the observation area as he operated on people. To say she idolized him would be an understatement.

When Loyal Davis died, Nancy had been at his bedside for days. Nancy's father died quietly one August morning and Nancy stayed with him and mourned. She didn't want her father moved until her brother could arrive from the East Coast. After that, the only thing left was to make the sad trip to her mother's home to tell her. Edie was wheelchair bound by then and suffering from early signs of dementia.

I had asked Dick Davis where he thought that Nancy's protectiveness came from. I expected him to bolster my opinion that it rose out of the insecurity of those years when her mother was on the road and she was left with her aunt and uncle. But he said he was sure that Nancy's behavior exactly mirrored the example set by her mother. Dick said Edie was very protective of Loyal Davis throughout their marriage; she would brook no criticism of him. "If you should dare, the wrath of Edie came down upon you," Dick explained with amusement in his voice.

While Edie Davis had limited her acting career when she married Loyal and moved Nancy to Chicago, she did occasionally participate on a local radio program with a young broadcaster named Mike Wallace. Mike loved telling stories about Edie's "lively" sense of humor. That was Mike's way of saying that Edie loved a dirty joke.

My favorite story about Edie centered on when she and Dr. Davis, along with the extended Reagan family, were staying at Blair House in the days leading up to the 1981 inauguration.

Legend has it that Edie was just pulling herself up out of the bathtub when a Secret Service agent mistakenly opened the door. You can imagine that his life must have passed before his eyes as he saw his career aspirations come crashing down. The spritely Mrs. Davis looked at him and said, "Well, young man, now you are going to have to marry me."

Years ago, one of the Reagans' LA friends, film producer A. C. Lyles, told me that when Edie visited the Reagans, she

constantly embarrassed her daughter by telling ribald jokes to their guests. He said he could still hear Nancy say, "Mother! Please!," horrified each time Edie indulged in sharing the latest vulgar jokes with the assembled and adoring guests. I suspect Nancy secretly enjoyed watching her mother entertain their friends.

Every time Nancy flew west she stopped in Phoenix to visit her mother in the Biltmore Estates. In later years, as her dementia worsened, Edie insisted on wearing red woolen gloves at all times regardless of the weather. Nancy catered to her every need when she was visiting and made careful arrangements to keep her comfortable in her absence. When her mother died, Nancy kept those red woolen gloves.

When my own mother died in the late 1980s, Nancy sent me a touching note of sympathy, saying she knew how hard it was to lose your mother because it meant you were nobody's child anymore. That was how she really felt about losing her mother.

Nancy was especially close to her niece, Ann Davis Peterson, who lived in the Washington area and was a frequent visitor to her aunt's temporary home on Pennsylvania Avenue. Dick Davis describes his daughter as a very positive, happy person with three great sons. He said Nancy loved Ann's company; they talked about "girl things."

The Reagan children each had strong personalities. Maureen was close to her father and she worked hard and successfully to develop a good relationship with Nancy. Maureen lived in the White House for about a year during the close of the Reagan presidency while she was working at the Republican National Committee. Maureen's brother, Michael, had become a strong conservative voice on radio, not dissimilar to the early career path of his dad who started out as a sportscaster.

Neither Patti nor Ron Jr. had much use for staff. They avoided us like the plague. And frankly, I didn't blame them. I suspected they saw us as a wedge between them and their parents. And after all the years their dad had spent in public life, they had to be tired of the omnipresent staff. It has to be difficult to be the children of a president when you have ambitions of your own to pursue.

When I step back and try to observe the children through the lens of time, it becomes obvious they all struggled to have their own identities. In the end, they each worked in areas that reflected their parents' identities—Republican activist Maureen, broadcasters Michael and Ron, and actress and author Patti.

When both Ron and Patti spoke at their mother's memorial service, the room was still. Between the two of them, their eulogies were the perfect balance between sorrow and joy. They truly rose to the occasion and I could feel their mother's pride.

I thought about something Nancy told me after President Reagan's services were concluded at the Reagan Library at sunset. She said she dreaded more than anything else going back alone to their empty house. But Ron and Patti took her home, brought in some pizza, and they all sat at the kitchen counter, eating pizza and talking. Nancy told me that story with love in her voice. She said it made all the difference.

I suspect Nancy had been reminded that she needed her children as much as they needed her. Maybe more. They completed the circle.

9

Christmas at the White House

I have never known anyone who loved the Christmas season more than Nancy Reagan. The busier the better. And the more traditional the better.

It's a good thing she so loved Christmas because, believe it or not, we had to begin serious planning for Christmas in August. Honest. Many of the national magazines planned and printed issues months in advance, which meant every August we had a day when the president and Nancy had to pretend it was Christmas. They dressed in their winter best and posed for color pictures in a room decorated for the holiday. You'd never know it was 100 degrees outside. The president, with all he had on his plate, always was unfailingly patient and polite while posing for endless "one more shot" requests in his red wool blazer.

Every December 25 during my years as her press secretary, I intruded on the presidential Christmas by calling to coax Nancy into giving me some good information about President and Mrs. Reagan's holiday. I would have a checklist in front of me: What did Nancy give Ronnie and vice versa? What members of the family were there? What was the menu for Christmas dinner? For the media, who were duty bound to report as many details as possible, no morsel was too small.

Since their days as young parents in California the Reagans had spent every Christmas Eve with their good friends Charlie and Mary Jane Wick. During the presidency the couples celebrated at the Wicks' Watergate apartment, and later at their home in DC. Their tradition was that a different person dressed as Santa every year, so I needed to know who played the part.

The Reagans always celebrated Christmas Day at the White House, rather than at Camp David or in California, because they wanted their protective detail to be able to spend Christmas with their families. They would leave for California the next day.

After I squeezed every bit of information out of Nancy, she returned to Christmas dinner and I briefed the wire services. Once that obligation was fulfilled, I was able to turn my attention to my own family Christmas. The press wasn't interested in my Christmas but my kids certainly were.

At first it was not easy to convince the Reagans of the import of my inquiries, but after seeing how the details were covered by news media across the country and realizing Americans really do like to know about their president's Christmas, they accepted my intrusions.

* * *

Whenever I find myself beginning to feel overwhelmed by all the work that goes into planning for our family Christmas, I remember what Nancy Reagan faced each year at the White House and how beautifully and graciously she handled the details.

In the first year, 1981, Christmas began with Nancy accepting delivery of a massive Christmas tree at 10:00 a.m. on December 2. Every year a different state is honored to provide the White House with its tree; and it always arrives at the North Portico in a horse-drawn wagon.

Once the tree arrived, the White House was closed to tours while professional florists and young people from a nearby drug treatment program decorated the tree. Nancy joined in the fun, helping hang ornaments.

On the afternoon of December 6, the Reagans stood with the White House social aides for their annual Christmas photo before they left for the traditional Kennedy Center Honors. You may have watched this wonderful program on television. The Reagans hosted an afternoon reception at the White House to kick off the "Honors" and they never missed going to this event where awardees from every aspect of the arts are honored. Nancy always said it felt like the official beginning of Christmas.

On December 7, at 11:00 a.m. Nancy unveiled the Christmas decorations for the press. The chef made a wonderful gingerbread house that graced the State Dining Room while the tree filled the Blue Room. Then at 2:00 p.m., the Reagans posed again with the tree for *Newsweek* magazine.

The afternoon of December 8 was devoted to an interview with *Newsweek* and more Christmas-themed photography. At

6:30 p.m. that same day the Reagans welcomed White House volunteers to a holiday reception to personally thank them for all their work during the year.

On Monday, December 14, Nancy hosted a Christmas party for the children of the diplomatic corps, an annual event much anticipated by those families.

That evening, the Reagans hosted the first of two back-to-back Christmas parties for the media. This broke from the tradition of one party. The change gave rise to the rumor that there must be an A list party and a B list party. Who says the White House press corps isn't a bit paranoid? The change was made only because the event had grown so large it wasn't fun for anyone. By breaking it into two events, media got to spread out around the State Floor, go through the official receiving line, and have drinks and wonderful food while enjoying the decor. We took our final guest list in alphabetical order and invited every other person (and guest) to alternate parties. And in a number of cases I had to explain that to a few members of the always suspicious media.

Ten days to go! On December 15 Nancy hosted a holiday party specifically for deaf children in the East Room and later that night we held the second press Christmas party, hopefully putting to permanent rest the rumor about one party being better than the other.

At 11:00 a.m. on December 16, I took the dean of the press corps, Helen Thomas of UPI, up to the private residence for an interview with Nancy and, what she was really after, a large version of that year's White House Christmas card. Helen collected them for years.

On December 17, President and Mrs. Reagan lit the na-

tional Christmas tree at the annual Pageant of Peace ceremony on the Ellipse near the Washington Monument. That
moment was televised across the country. An hour later they
held a Christmas reception for the Secret Service.

The calendar for December 20 shows the Reagans going
to an 11:00 a.m. church service. Early afternoon they taped
a television program with Young American Artists at the
White House, followed by attending a party for their senior
staff. Christmas was still five days away.

On Monday, December 21, Nancy invited her East Wing
staff to the residence for what became an annual Christmas
party. That was the last official event of the week.

The Reagans never seemed tired. They both seemed to
know how important these social events were to folks who
had worked hard all year and how much pride everyone felt in
bringing their families to meet the president and First Lady at
the gloriously decorated White House.

* * *

I haven't even mentioned the Christmas cards yet. The Reagans, like all modern-day presidential families, sent out thousands of Christmas cards—in the range of sixty thousand.
The master list, as I recall, was kept by folks at the Republican National Committee. The RNC also footed the bill for
the annual mass mailing. The Christmas cards were always
made in the USA and every year that I remember, Gibson and
Hallmark—the only two American greeting card companies
left—fought hard for the honor to make the president's Christmas card. I was thrilled to be given the enlarged versions of
all eight of the Reagan cards.

The first is still my favorite. Jamie Wyeth painted the back of the White House at night after a blanket of snow had fallen (entitled "Christmas Eve at the White House") with only one light on. It was Nancy's dressing room light where I could picture her wrapping last-minute gifts.

My second favorite was their 1984 card, also by Wyeth. It was the front of the White House in snow at Christmas with meandering paw prints of a barely discernible squirrel making his way to the majestic North Portico. I suspect it was a nod from the artist to President Reagan's daily ritual of leaving acorns outside the Oval Office every morning for our resident squirrels.

For their second card, artist James Steinmeyer, a young illustrator known particularly for his interiors, was selected to paint Nancy's favorite, the Red Room. When I look at it, I honestly feel like I am standing there in that beautiful room.

In 1983 the Green Room was the focus, this time honoring New York illustrator Mark Hampton with the commission. His work is watercolors in fine detail. To me, it's magical.

The Blue Room was painted by Thomas William Jones for the 1985 card—again with incredible detail. Jones was asked to paint the cards for the next three years, featuring the East Room in 1986 where your eye is drawn to the Gilbert Stuart painting of George Washington. For the 1987 card, the artist moved into the historic State Dining Room where Abraham Lincoln pensively surveys the room. The last Reagan card in 1988 is also by Jones. It features the cross hall where guests arriving at the North Portico enter the State Floor. Here, in this hall, the Marine Corps band plays and guests dance at the end of the evening after a memorable state dinner. I once watched Princess Diana dancing there with the president.

Every year I'd ask Nancy which card she liked best. She just smiled and said she loved them all. Though I think she had to have loved that first card best.

For the rest of my years in Washington, whenever I drove by the back of the White House, I'd glance up at that dressing room window and remember those Christmases.

* * *

One Christmas—1984—stands out as the best.

Amie Garrison's parents were desperate. Time was running out for their five-year-old daughter, Amie, who was unlikely to be alive on Christmas without a new liver.

Dr. Tom Starzl from the University of Pittsburgh Medical Center called Nancy to tell her about the urgent need to find a liver for this child. Nancy knew Tom because her father, neurosurgeon Loyal Davis, had been involved in Starzl's early surgical training. In fact, Dr. Starzl said he learned more about surgery from Loyal Davis in three months at Northwestern than he thought possible. He called Nancy and, as only she could, the First Lady set the wheels in motion for an incredible ten days.

Nancy Reagan invited the Garrisons to bring Amie to the White House on December 10, 1984, when she was scheduled to take the press corps on a tour of the Christmas decorations.

She surprised the press when she wheeled in a tiny little girl whose skin was a deep yellow and introduced her to the media. Amie helped Nancy put ornaments on the tree while cameras flashed. Nancy explained to the press the urgent need to find a liver for this child. She knew the story would become the centerpiece of their coverage and attract a great deal of attention.

Ten days later, thanks to the massive, worldwide publicity, a donor liver was found in Canada. But the University of Pittsburgh's operating rooms were booked solid.

The team of Starzl and Reagan kept the pressure on. Dr. Starzl called Dr. John Fordtran, chief of internal medicine at Baylor in Dallas, and said he wanted to come to Baylor to perform the transplant. Starzl had been working with Baylor to set up a transplant center there, but it was several months away from its scheduled opening under the leadership of Baylor's Dr. Göran Klintmalm.

For Baylor the stakes could not have been higher, but after heavy debate there was 100 percent agreement that Amie's life was at stake and they would respond accordingly. Then it got even more complicated. Dr. Starzl had to call on Nancy to help his team, sitting on an airport tarmac in Canada with the donor liver on ice, to get their plane cleared to take off. Done. Then the White House had to intervene again to get them cleared for priority landing at Love Field in Dallas. Done. Time was of the essence.

I talked with both Amie and her father about the experience.

Gerry Garrison, Amie's dad, knows his daughter would not be here, alive and well thirty-four years later, with three children of her own, had Dr. Starzl and Nancy Reagan not worked so hard to save her life. He said the Garrisons were sitting on a plane waiting to take off for Pittsburgh when they heard the news that the surgery was being moved to Dallas. The surgery itself took sixteen hours. Amie's dad said the waiting was the hardest. Waiting for a liver; waiting for the surgery to take place. He said for so long "we waited, we hoped, we wished, we prayed" for Amie to get a liver.

Amie was transported from Dallas back to Pittsburgh for a recovery period, and while they were there Amie's parents met with the parents of a three-year-old boy who had died in an auto accident; it was his liver that was giving Amie a chance to live.

The Garrisons grieved with the Canadian parents who'd lost their son. Amie, the center of all this attention, says she was "too young" and too sick to remember any of the drama that swirled around her.

The impact of Nancy's personal intervention was profound. When you can help people save lives, people never forget. They know you care. You are also changed in meaningful ways. Nancy Reagan, First Lady, saved lives. I think it really changed her.

Dr. Starzl died March 4, 2017, a year after Nancy passed away. I'd left an email message for him a week before hoping I could talk to him about Amie and Nancy. Several days later I read his obituary; that same day an email reply popped up under his name. I was startled to see Tom Starzl's name there in my in-box and I looked at it a few moments before opening it. Of course, it was from his office assistant making sure I knew about his passing. But for just a moment, I couldn't help hoping it was from him.

All I could think about as I gathered the material for this story was that the good doctor and the determined First Lady had been quite a team. Nancy's dad, the exacting surgeon Loyal Davis, would be proud of them both. Lives well lived.

◄

10

The Art Lover

The eclectic list of performers who graced the White House during the eight Reagan years is thirty-five pages long, and every page sparkles with the names of legends. And Nancy was the artistic "engine" that drove the glittering entertainment in the Reagan White House.

The legendary artists ranged from Abracadabra, the magician who performed for the Diplomatic Children's Party, to violinist Pinchas Zukerman and his then wife, Eugenia, on the flute who performed at the state dinner for Pakistan.

Here is a small sample of the dazzling array of performers who graced the Reagan White House:

Eddie Albert, June Allison, Bea Arthur
Burt Bachrach, Pearl Bailey, the Beach Boys, Tony Bennett, Dave
Brubeck, George Burns
Perry Como
Ella Fitzgerald, Roberta Flack, Pete Fountain

The Gatlin Brothers, Dizzy Gillespie, Mickey Gilley, Benny
Goodman, Robert Goulet
Gene Kelly
Peggy Lee, Rich Little
Johnny Mathis, Zubin Mehta, Robert Merrill, Liza Minnelli
Bob Newhart
Bobby Short, Beverly Sills, Frank Sinatra
Mr. T, Frank Tate
Dionne Warwick, Andy Williams
All the magnificent military bands

You'll see the name "Frank Tate" right after Mr. T on the list of artists. Frank happens to be my dear brother-in-law who is an accomplished bassist, playing for many years with Pearl Bailey and then Bobby Short at the Carlyle Hotel. It was a thrill for the Tate family every time he performed at the White House while I was working there.

Nancy was so proud of the willingness of all these performers to give their time and talent to entertain at the nation's house. And she loved the diversity of the performing arts represented on the White House stage.

* * *

The popular PBS program *In Performance at the White House* was one of Nancy's favorites. Many of the stars of the program, who used the White House as their stage, were part of the *Young American Artists in Performance at the White House*, a four-part series taped in the East Room.

Nancy Reagan was genuinely enthusiastic about the idea of

bringing together some of the great maestros of our time and some of our nation's most promising young artists. In opening remarks before one of these performances, Nancy said she knew "no better or more enjoyable way to emphasize that the White House is the national home of all Americans than through a series of performances by young artists here in the East Room."

I came across one letter addressed to President Reagan that expresses beautifully the widespread appreciation Americans had for the *Young American Artists in Performance* series. It was dated Christmas Eve 1981.

> *Dear President Reagan,*
>
> *I just listened to your White House program with Beverly Sills and her young singers. Thank you so much for making it possible for us to listen to that beautiful program. I cried it was so wonderful. And your nice speech afterwards, and the Christmas carols honoring our Lord were grand. I rejoiced to hear it.*
>
> *You will no doubt get many letters, and some of great importance, but I want to add my small voice of approval of what you are attempting to do for our Country. I am behind you all the way in words and prayers. We need men like you, as the poet says: "Men, sun crowned, who stand above the crowd in public duty and in private thinking."*

The press also enjoyed covering these musical programs at the White House. It is amazing how those steely-eyed political reporters became starry-eyed groupies in the presence of the great entertainers. I vividly recall wire service reporters

Helen Thomas and Maureen Santini, along with Donnie Radcliffe of the *Washington Post*, getting all giggly when they were able to talk with Perry Como and Rock Hudson.

Both Nancy and the president looked forward to the entertainment. Nancy usually slipped into the East Room the afternoon of a scheduled program when the entertainers were rehearsing. I recall one time when Roberta Flack was rehearsing. Nancy stood in the Red Room next door with one door ajar so she could listen without disturbing Roberta.

When Sinatra came to the White House, he never wanted to be present when media were around. He simply didn't trust them and definitely did not want to talk with them. He was the polar opposite of Perry Como, who loved talking with everyone. Nancy and the president loved having Sinatra as their resource for picking entertainment; he had, as you can imagine, significant clout with a whole range of entertainers.

I always provided the media with a guest list in advance of a state dinner. Early in the evening, as guests were arriving, they came in through the Diplomatic Reception Room where a harpist played music to welcome them. Then they had to walk past a long rope line of reporters and cameras. If you were a senator or congressman or a member of the senior staff at the White House, you seldom even got asked a question. Occasionally someone would snap a picture. But if a big name baseball player came through, as occasionally happened, at least six male reporters would whip out a baseball and ask for his autograph, just like kids.

The press always enjoyed the formal entertainment in the East Room. That was at the end of the evening for them. Once they left, guests danced to the Marine Band musicians in the Grand Foyer. Only the official photographers were allowed for those final moments. That's when guests like Princess Diana would really cut a rug. The evening drew to a close when the president and Nancy moved into the foyer and made their way to the elevator to take them upstairs to the residence. I personally enjoyed watching people begin to leave through the "front" door, more formally known as the North Portico, because you could read their emotions as they left. They didn't want to forget a moment of the evening. They would pause and look out toward Pennsylvania Avenue, then at each other and smile. Like clockwork. It made all our work feel worthwhile. Of course, then I'd look at the clock and head for my car, hoping to be home by midnight since the next day started somewhere between 6:00 and 7:00 a.m.

Throughout the years of the Reagan presidency, Nancy continued to use the White House "stage" as an influential platform for American arts and artists. It should always be so.

11

Finding Her Voice

If you were paying attention during the Reagan years, there was a visible change in Nancy Reagan during the first couple of years of the presidency. I watched her transform from a hesitant, ill-at-ease speaker to an effective, confident communicator. She went from giving only short, impersonal remarks to speaking at length on emotional subjects as she became comfortable being personal and passionate in front of an audience. Over time, Nancy realized that it was more convincing to reveal her passions than to speak in generalities. Once a First Lady recognizes her power to influence opinions, she learns to draw her audience in and, before they know it, make them her allies.

Early in 1981 she met with the East Wing press contingent for the first time. These were the female reporters—not a male among them—who would follow her closely and be writing about her regularly. The press was pressuring me to arrange a meeting. Nancy was quite nervous and only agreed to meet with them if we limited the time and the subject matter. She told them a bit about her commitment to the Foster Grandparent Program using language she had repeated so often she didn't have to think hard about what she was saying. She gave a short, prepared talk, thanked the ladies, and left the room without taking any questions. She just wasn't ready yet. I felt like it was partly my fault, not having prepared her well enough. And I never made that mistake again.

By later that year, she was regularly visiting treatment and prevention programs for young people with drug problems. On those trips she began to loosen up, learning to listen to the people she met and respond to them directly. She also became increasingly more comfortable talking with the press. Gradually, her interaction with various reporters allowed her to become more confident every day.

I remember when, in the fall of 1982, she traveled to Alabama for the Governor's Conference on Drug Awareness. She asked her audience to think of Helen Keller who grew up in Alabama.

"Here was a girl whose young life was a void of silence and darkness; a void most of us cannot even comprehend. Yet there are children in this state today who are just as removed from the world, except that the void is inside them. Drugs have killed their hope, their promise, their spirit, their love. Drugs have turned them against their friends and families and toward a world of pain and isolation. . . .

"I'm told that your state motto is 'We Dare Defend Our Rights.' Well, what this conference is saying is we dare to defend our children."

Nancy was beginning to find her voice.

Not long after the Alabama conference, she addressed the first conference of the National Federation of Parents for Drug-Free Youth.

She opened her remarks by telling them she hoped this first conference would be their last due to their dogged determination to organize and educate the nation to fight youth drug abuse. If they did a good enough job, we could beat this scourge.

She then used a quote her staff began to enjoy listening for. She used it a lot. We kept count. "There is a saying a woman is like a tea bag—you never know her strength until she is in hot water."

And then in February 1983, Nancy spoke at the Heart Luncheon. This is one of the best speeches she ever gave and brings tears to my eyes every time I read it.

She began on a light note, mentioning how First Ladies today show their support for good causes like this one a little differently from our early First Ladies. Dolley Madison, for instance, supported the Washington Orphans Asylum by giving them $5 and a cow.

She went on to say: "You know there is a saying that when the heart is full, it's the eyes that overflow. I'll try to keep my eyes from overflowing today, but I can't promise, because I'd like to share something with you. To say that heart disease is the number one killer is such a vast statement, but when it strikes your own family, the statistic is suddenly so personal. As you may have read, my father died last August from heart failure. He was eighty-six and, despite the technical medical explanations, I think his loving heart simply wore out after a long, wonderful life. But I want to tell you why I am thankful, why I feel luckier than many whose loved ones die from heart disease.

"I had some last precious hours with my father. I tried to tell him how much he influenced my life and how deeply proud I was of his contributions to medicine. When he died, he just went to sleep, as if some twilight had overtaken him. And I feel so very thankful for having had the chance to say goodbye and tell him I loved him. There are so many who are taken from us without warning. Their families simply receive the terrible message and the hard reality that the person will never again come through the door.

"Apart from my husband, my father was the most important man in my life and heart disease took him away. As a gifted doctor, he believed deeply in the power of caring and in the potential of prevention, and these beliefs are also the very essence of the American Heart Association. . . ."

She ended this moving personal talk by telling the audience that she was writing an article about her father that would be appearing in the Father's Day issue of *McCall's* magazine and she would be donating the fee to the American Heart Association in memory of her father.

How Nancy Reagan had grown. To stand before a large audience and relive the final moments you had with your father takes real courage. As she used to say: "A woman is like a tea bag . . ." She proved how strong she was in so many ways over the years.

* * *

Nancy Reagan flew to Boys Town, Nebraska, in late November 1986 to accept an award for her campaign against youth drug abuse. Boys Town had been founded as an orphanage for boys run by Catholic priests and was the subject of a very popular movie classic, *Boys Town*. In 2017, Boys Town celebrated its centennial and is now sheltering children in facilities across the country. By the time Nancy traveled there, the home accepted both girls and boys. It was run by Father Peter.

With help again from speechwriter Landon Parvin, Nancy gave a short but powerful speech:

> Thank you for this distinguished award. I'm very honored. But, as Father Peter knows, the reason I'm here today is not because of the award, but because of you.
>
> I came all the way from Washington this morning so I could talk to you for five minutes. And I'll tell you the reason why. Because Father Peter told me that there have been times when you thought no one cared about you. I came today because I wanted you to know I care.
>
> To be cared for is what all of us want. And when we don't get that, it hurts. I know that you sometimes hurt inside. I know you wonder why things keep going wrong in your life. I know you sometimes feel confused and lonely and unsure where you belong.
>
> There was a time when I didn't quite know where I belonged, either. You see, when I was young, my mother was an actress and so she had to travel. I missed her and she missed me.
>
> My father left us, so I stayed with my aunt and uncle.

They were very good people but they weren't my parents. And what I wished for more than anything else in the world was a normal family. I finally got my wish when my mother married a wonderful man, who became my wonderful father. And at last I knew where I belonged.

I know you ask yourself where you belong, too. It's not easy being here in Boys Town with new faces and new ways of doing things. But isn't the pain you felt when you first came here less than the pain where you were before? And pain is what I want to talk to you about for a minute.

Do you know what happens when you hurt inside? You usually start closing your heart to people. Because that's how you got hurt in the first place—you opened your heart.

Another thing that happens is that you stop trusting people. Because somewhere along the way they probably didn't live up to your trust.

And there's another thing that happens when you've been hurt. You start to think you're not worth much. You think to yourself "Well, how can I be worth anything, if someone would treat me in this terrible way?"

So, I understand why you feel beaten down by it all. Some of you may have tried drugs in order to escape those feelings. But, please, believe me, drugs aren't the answer. They'll only make the pain worse in the long run. It's pretty hard to imagine that you can hurt worse than you did before you came here, but it's true. Whatever anyone has done to you, drugs will make it worse.

Boys Town is your fresh start. No matter why you're

here. No matter what you've suffered. No matter what you've done. If you work at it, you can be free of your troubles. You can be anything you want to be. And you can be happy. But you have to open your heart just a little. You have to trust just a little and begin to believe in yourself.

I believe in you. I'm proud of you already. Because when you came to Boys Town, you signed a paper that you wanted to be here. Whether you realized it or not, that was your way of saying that you believed life can get better. And it can. And all the family—teachers and all the staff and all the facilities of Boys Town are here to help give you a clean start. Boys Town is a wish that takes a little work. But you have to do the work. Because it's your life.

I hope we will see each other again, but if we don't I want you to remember something long after I leave here today, and it's this.

I believe in you. I believe in what you can do. I believe you are important and deserve the very best that life can offer.

And although someone is sitting beside you or in front of you right now, I'm saying this to each one of you alone—I'm saying it just to you. And I hope you'll always remember it. I know how good you are inside and I would be proud to call you my own.

I am certain that not a single day of the year goes by without some of you, or even all of you, giving thanks that there was a Father Flanagan and that there is a Boys Town.

I asked Landon what he remembers about that day. He said, "You don't think about kids being emotionally moved but I know I saw kids wiping their noses on their sleeves and using their shirttails for the tears in their eyes." He also said that Father Peter told him he could live for a full year on what she had told the kids, using it in his talks with them, reminding them of what she said.

For me, thinking back to how timid she was meeting the East Wing press for the first time, fearful of answering questions, feeling like nobody in that room liked her, I was amazed and moved by how far she'd come.

* * *

During those years Nancy would hand me a fat pile of index cards held together with a rubber band. She suggested I look them over and see if we could use them as a model for one of her future speeches.

Until recently those cards were among my files in my basement filing cabinet. I cannot recall our ever using them as a speech template and I do not remember why. I think it's likely that I never managed to look at them while in the White House and forgot all about them.

These cards—about ninety of them—date back to the president's time as California governor, making them more than fifty years old. They were typewritten transcriptions of letters he received from schoolkids. He had apparently suggested Nancy read them to see if she could use them at luncheons to amuse her various audiences in Sacramento. She may have done that. They reminded me of the popular TV show *Kids Say the Darndest Things*.

Now of course I've left out everything to do with our private life. Well it's pretty normal — like sending our son to camp for the 1st time & the long anxious wait for that 1st letter & then it came. (14)

```
     Dear Mom and Dad:

          I arrived O.K.  Mike barfed on the

     plane.

                         Love,

                         Ronnie
```

(16)

And last — the inevitable question about the press & how we see it. Well I've overheard my husband doing his own editorializing — in the shower but I also know he agrees with Thomas Jefferson.

After waiting on pins and needles to hear from Ron, their son, at his first sleep-away camp, the note finally arrived. It was about his friend, Mike, who apparently got airsick on the plane.

Even more interesting, Governor Reagan had edited them in his handwriting, and Nancy, in several instances, had edited his edits. One of my favorites was from Maria in third grade.

And then a letter to think about and wonder what takes place between 3rd grade & some of our so called higher ed.

(##)

```
     Dear Governor,

          I am a new citizen.  My whole family is         15

     too.  We come from Mexico.

          More than anything I want a great

     American flag.  I will love and care for it.

               Your new friend who loves you,

                         Maria

          P.S.  I will also treat it with respect.
```

This note was from a third grader named Maria, a recent citizen from Mexico. She wanted her own American flag, promising to treat it with respect. Governor Reagan added a suggested comment for Nancy to make about this note, wondering about what happened to the quality of teaching between third grade and higher education.

She told him that she and her whole family had recently become citizens.

> "We come from Mexico," she wrote, and "more than anything I want a great American flag. I will love and care for it." She signed it: "Your new friend who loves you."

I have sent these cards to Joanne Drake at the Reagan Library where they belong.

* * *

As year seven of the Reagan administration reached its midpoint, Nancy went to New York and addressed the American Newspaper Publishers Luncheon at the Waldorf Astoria. In 1981 she would never have even considered this, but by 1987 she was a different First Lady. Sit back and enjoy.

"I was afraid I might have to cancel. You know how busy I am—between staffing the White House and overseeing the arms talks.

"In fact, this morning I had planned to clear up US–Soviet differences on intermediate range nuclear missiles ... but I decided to clean out Ronnie's sock drawer instead.

"You know I recently read that I am an 'unelected, unaccountable' 'power-hungry' 'political manipulator' of 'extraordinary vindictiveness' who 'is supported in her power playing by a bloated, expensive East Wing staff, exhibits a zest for combat and presumes to control the actions and appointments of the executive branch.'

"As my son said, 'Yeah, Mom, that's you.'"

She talked about how naive she was that first year.

"I read that I wanted the Carters to move out of the White House early; that I banned sumo wrestlers from the Rose Garden; that I planned to tear down a wall in the Lincoln bedroom."

She went on to say: "But what I finally began to realize was this: As First Lady, you will be the object of attention no matter what you do. So, I decided I might as well focus the attention on something that really mattered, on something that had interested me for a long time and on which I'd already started having briefings—the problem of drug abuse among our young people."

She used her spotlight to good effect. She traveled to sixty cities in thirty-one states and seven foreign countries to raise awareness of the issue. And she traveled several hundred thousand miles in the process.

"Every mile, every meeting has been worth it. My work against drugs has provided me with the most fulfilling years of my life," Nancy said.

Later in the speech, she talked at length about her husband as an individual.

"A president has advisers to counsel him on foreign affairs, on defense, on the economy, on politics, on any number of matters. But no one among all those experts is there to look after him as an individual with human needs, as a flesh-and-blood person who must deal with the pressures of holding the most powerful position on earth."

She told them that she was a woman who loves her husband. "I have opinions. He has opinions. We don't always agree. But neither marriage nor politics denies a spouse the right to hold an opinion or the right to express it."

She talked about advice she'd give to the next First Lady.

"First, be yourself. There will be plenty of smart advisers telling you this will be good for you or that will be good for you, but you have to do what you feel is best for yourself.

"Second, do what you're interested in. No one was enthusiastic about my getting involved in the drug problem. They thought it was too grim and depressing.

"Third, don't be afraid to look after your husband or to voice your opinions, either to him or his staff.

"Fourth, once you're in the White House don't think it's going to be a glamorous, fairy-tale life. It's very hard work with high highs and low lows.

"And fifth, my last piece of advice is this: Never wear a ring on your right hand in a receiving line—it's always a little old lady who will squeeze so hard she'll bring you to your knees."

She ended quoting Albert Schweitzer: "One thing I know: the only ones among you who will be really happy are those who will have found how to serve."

"Well," she said, "I am very happy because I have been given the chance to really serve. The peaks are worth the valleys a hundred times over. And I want the American people to know I am honored to be their First Lady."

And I was honored to be a member of her staff.

12

Press Contacts

Nancy was wary of the press. She'd been disappointed by experiences with national media when her husband was California governor. Her friends thought Nancy never fully recovered from the nasty piece Joan Didion wrote about her when Ronald Reagan was governor of California. She'd been burned during the campaign, too. One day Nancy walked down the aisle of the campaign plane and offered candy to members of the press. Judy Bachrach, with the *Washington Post*, wrote a snotty story about Nancy pushing candy on everyone and mentioned that Nancy had "piano legs." I am told that Nancy cried when she read that article.

Most of the women reporters covering politics were and are liberals; some seemed to have a visceral dislike for women who didn't fit that mold. If you weren't for the Equal Rights Amendment and abortion rights, you were a traitor to your gender. Given her history with the press and their assumptions about her, it's no wonder she was skeptical of them.

As reporters covering Nancy got to know me, I was surprised by how many of them said something to the effect, "Sheila, you're different; you are a reasonable person." They had no idea what my political beliefs were; they just assumed because I was friendly and helpful, I must be at least a moderate if not a liberal Republican. I never disabused them of their characterization; it helped Nancy's coverage. The truth is that I am a fairly conservative Republican who grew up in a Democratic family. We have differing political views but we love one another. It is possible, even in this highly polarized universe.

I remember early in the Reagan presidency when an AP reporter, Ann Blackman, interviewed Nancy outside on the lawn. Ann was getting nothing in the way of interesting comments until I steered her toward asking about Nancy's husband's role as a father. Father's Day was looming and it seemed like a good opportunity. Nancy really opened up and Ann got herself a decent story. Nancy never liked to talk about herself but, as this instance proved to me, she relaxed and talked freely about people or things she cared about.

I never ceased to be amazed at how many false rumors circulated about the First Lady. Or how some news outlets let politics dominate the tone of their coverage from the beginning.

Deputy Press Secretary Barbara Cook Fabiani handed me a message one spring day in 1982 that was a real doozy. Patricia Avery, *US News & World Report*, heard from a "good" source that Nancy was having a hysterectomy in June at George Washington University Hospital.

When I called Nancy to make an official inquiry, she

roared laughing. Her response, once she could stop laughing, was, "No, I think I want to try for one more pregnancy but don't tell the press."

Tish Avery was a good reporter so I am sure she dumped that "good" source.

In the early days of the Reagan administration, Donnie Radcliffe, *Washington Post* Style reporter, asked for a list of the most frequently asked questions I got about Nancy from the press:

What is she wearing?

How much does that (anything) cost?

Who is paying for it?

Will Frank Sinatra be there?

What kind of bed do the Reagans sleep in?

What brand of jelly beans do the Reagans prefer?

Does the president snore?

What size shirt does the president wear?

Does Nancy wear a bulletproof vest?

What do the Reagans eat?

When do they eat it?

Upon what dishes?

Donnie ended her "Washington Ways" column with this line: "Next week, maybe, the answers." Not likely. I was much more interested in changing the nature of questions we got. Eventually we succeeded. Over time, people wanted to know more about the Foster Grandparent Program, and about programs to treat youth with drug abuse problems. But they always wanted recipes of the favorite presidential food.

* * *

Early in 1981, Nina Hyde of the *Washington Post* reported that Nancy's recent sightings in a fox-collared shrug and a mink coat has spurred an animal rights group to request a meeting with the First Lady to discuss the issue, and that we were ignoring the request.

Nancy called our chief of staff, Peter McCoy, concerned about the "fur people" we'd been fending off. She wondered if we couldn't explain to them that her mink was a ranch mink, meaning the varmints had been raised on a ranch for this purpose. Peter, who had a wonderful sense of humor, said he thought they were concerned more with the minks' demise than where they grew up. Peter's humor helped get us through a lot of stressful days.

It fell to me to hear the concerns of the animal rights advocates. I gingerly raised the question as to whether or not they distinguished "a ranch mink from other fur-bearing animals" to which their representative replied, "That would be racism in the animal kingdom."

Nancy was never seen wearing the coat in public again during her eight years in the White House. And most important, the fur coat never caught on as a big issue with the press. After I left the White House in 1985 and could afford it, I bought a lovely, warm mink coat. My personal protest.

* * *

I had to Just Say No to Reagan friend Ray Stark, the producer of *Annie* on Broadway. Nancy was going to the opening at his invitation. She sent me in advance to walk through his plans.

And it was a good thing she did. Ray had a "strong" personality, and I knew I needed to be ready for anything.

His plans included having Nancy in a basement elevator that would come from below and open center stage releasing a foggy mist through which Nancy would magically and majestically appear. I said no, she wanted to arrive like everyone else and slide quietly into her seat.

I swear I saw some of that foggy mist coming out of Ray's ears. He did not buy into my explanation that the media would treat Nancy badly if we gave them any opportunity. She wanted everything low-key.

I explained it all to Nancy and she agreed with my decision and backed me up. I am certain Ray called her within an hour of our meeting to demand I be fired.

In truth, well-meaning friends can cause great embarrassment in circumstances like this. We had to always be alert to this kind of over-the-top plan.

* * *

The single most important person in the First Lady's press office was Betsy Koons Robertson. She was with the press office the entire eight years, working her way up from our executive assistant to deputy press secretary. She kept everything on schedule. No one worked harder.

Betsy was even Nancy's stand-in for one memorable event in 1988. The First Lady was scheduled to attend a Just Say No rally for kids during halftime of the Indiana Pacers versus Philadelphia 76ers game to highlight her antidrug education program. Philadelphia's Charles Barkley and the Pacers Wayman Tisdale were supposed to lift Nancy up to dunk a basketball.

Our perfectionist advance man insisted on a rehearsal using Betsy as Nancy's stand-in. Betsy found herself being lifted by her heels up to the imaginary net by these two huge fellows; she performed perfectly. Even though she admits she was a nervous wreck.

Nancy performed perfectly later that day when the well-rehearsed basketball players lifted her exactly as planned. The creative way Nancy brought attention to Just Say No drew a great deal of media attention that night. As I always preached to my clients, a picture really is worth a thousand words.

Betsy was typically sweet and soft-spoken, but I remember one time when she ripped into our Chinese counterparts when we were at the Children's Palace in Shanghai watching a children's performance. Unbeknownst to us, during the dance, the American press bus was moved by our hosts from its assigned spot at the end of the motorcade. As a result, the press missed the motorcade and we had some very unhappy scribes. To make matters worse, Betsy was literally running around the property trying to find the bus. The Chinese got an earful after that.

These are the kinds of snafus Nancy never knew about. Unless we regaled her with stories about all the behind-the-scenes drama of these events much later. She loved hearing these tales—after the fact when they were no longer a problem.

I never told her about one memorable incident. In the early '80s, White House staffers carried very heavy pagers wherever they went. They buzzed at first, quickly followed by a voice calling out your last name. Imagine having your purse call out "Tate, Tate" while you were standing in the checkout line at Safeway one night after work. When it happened to me one particular night, I raced out of the store, found the pay phone, inserted my quarter, and called in to find Nancy wanted to ask me several questions about something I had proposed. It took quite a while to bring the call to an end. Nancy had no idea I was standing outside in the pouring rain. I never told her. And, in hindsight, one might ask why I didn't tell her I was standing in the rain and would go home and call her right back. Duty, honor, country.

Speaking of country, on July 5, 1986, Nancy, accompanied by one hundred French and American schoolchildren, participated in the official reopening of the Statue of Liberty to the public. Hordes of media from around the world were in attendance.

As Betsy tells the story, "Nancy put her foot down and overruled her Secret Service agents when they opposed her plan to go all the way up to the crown with two of the children to officially reopen the iconic statue."

Nancy put great credence in the recommendations of her agents and she trusted them entirely. In this rare case, she knew how symbolically important the picture of America's First Lady with one French and one American child was. It sent a powerful message that reminded the people of our two nations of their historic bonds of friendship. Not to mention, the press photographers loved her for doing it.

* * *

It's easy to forget how much gossip made its way into the news during that period. In those days, every daily newspaper had a gossip columnist and the weekly newsmagazines had a gossip page. One of the aspects of my job that I disliked was my obligation to feed tidbits to these columnists.

The Queen of Gossip in the '80s was Diana McLellan. Her column, "The Ear," was very popular. It became a staple of the *Washington Post* after the *Washington Star* closed up shop. I once asked her, with exasperation in my voice, why she didn't come to me for verification of an item before she published incorrect stories. Diana readily and cheerily admitted that she didn't want the facts to get in the way of a good story. She was such a character it was hard to stay mad at her.

Betty Beale was the queen of Washington society reporters. She and her column reigned supreme from the '50s through the '80s. She expected, and she got, a good deal of special treatment to keep her writing favorable pieces. I even had to make sure she had a special parking space when she came to cover state dinners. Those days, when private dinners were peopled by the Washington elite, Betty took discreet notes and wrote flattering items about the hostess. I took good care of Betty because she always took good care of Nancy, at least as long as Betty felt she was getting the attention she deserved.

One of my favorite "social" reporters was Susan Watters. She wrote for *Women's Wear Daily*, the bible of the American fashion industry. She didn't cover politics, as you can imagine. One evening, after a state dinner, she and I walked out the front doors onto the iconic North Portico at the same time as one of the guests. Susan, looking for more social gossip, looked at him and asked, "Who are you?" It was Henry Cabot Lodge, former US senator from Massachusetts, US ambassador to the United Nations, to South Vietnam, and to West Germany. Not to mention he was the Republican candidate for vice president in 1960. He was "Mr. Republican." I tried to pretend I didn't know Susan at that moment. In truth, I loved her. She was great company. And an excellent writer.

A very tricky moment for me involved Bob Hope. He was a White House guest of the Reagans at a time that coincided with his eightieth birthday. Unbeknownst to Nancy, Bob had arranged (presumably through his publicists) to be interviewed by one of the networks while staying at 1600 Pennsylvania Avenue. When Nancy heard about it she called me in a tizzy. There is a long-standing tradition that no one was allowed to be interviewed by broadcasters in the White House except the president and First Lady. She told me to please help her, to "handle" it.

I called the network and we negotiated a deal whereby they would interview Bob in my office, which was technically in the White House, but they agreed not to identify the location during the interview nor were they to ask him any questions about where he was celebrating his birthday. The network agreed; Bob did the interview and the questions led him to reminisce about his life. Everyone was happy. I remember setting up the exact frame for the camera during the interview so there was nothing in the background to give the location away. Bob never knew what we'd done; he had a birthday interview; White House tradition was preserved.

One morning, there was an interesting article in one of the newspapers that caught my eye. It also dealt with the need to protect the image of the White House, in this case, specifically against commercial interests. A paragraph in the article read:

> "People keep stuffing them into their beaded evening bags and dinner jacket pockets to take home for souvenirs. So it's time for Nancy Reagan to reorder those oversized monogrammed damask dinner napkins that Jackie Kennedy started using at state dinners at the White House during the days of 'Camelot.' The price has doubled, to $900 a dozen, in the past 20 years."

My by-now practiced eye readily recognized the dinner napkin item for what it was. A clever way for the New York linen shop to gin up some business. Hostesses always wanted whatever the White House ordered. A stern warning went out through the White House Legal Office. No more bogus items about napkins showed up in the papers.

The real reason the White House needs to order new china every fifteen years or so is not breakage, which is rare indeed; it's politely called "loss." Some people simply cannot leave the White House where they have just had the privilege of dining without "losing" a saucer or a demitasse cup into their pocket. Since the mold for each china service is destroyed after it is delivered to the White House, the possibility of ordering replacement pieces is not an option. At one state dinner, Joan Rivers was a guest. She talked with Deputy Press Secretary Barbara Fabiani and me afterward and showed us all the items she'd been able to slip into her purse. Let the record show she did not take any china. She took name cards, menus, a few flowers; at least that's what she showed us.

* * *

As Nancy Reagan began to travel on her campaign against youth drug abuse, the gossip seemed to diminish and the press began to cover her seriously.

The influential *New York Times* reporter Maureen Dowd joined us in Atlanta in 1984 when Nancy went to a McDonald's to help launch the food chain's international drug prevention program. As Nancy walked up to order her meal, I told her it was very important to order a "Big Mac and a Coke." That was all the folks at McDonald's and Coca-Cola asked. I said it twice to make sure she understood. The TV cameras were ready and the sound was on.

Nancy went through the line and ordered a "Big Mac and an orange drink." The Coca-Cola management had lent us several of their employees to serve as "advance men" for this event. All they'd asked was a mention of Coca-Cola. Nancy blew it. Or she really just wanted an orange drink.

Maureen, unaware of my chagrin, duly reported what Nancy ordered and went on to write about how much more relaxed and open Nancy seemed.

I found the major media who covered Nancy Reagan to be pros. I almost never felt the need to complain. The photographers were even better to deal with. They simply wanted to do their jobs, to get a good picture. Only once, at a state dinner, did I have to intervene to keep two photographers from getting into fisticuffs.

Photographers are ushered into the State Dining Room to capture the toast made by the president in honor of his visitor. Many bring unwieldly stepladders into the room in order to climb as high as possible above the guests to get their picture. In this case, one American photographer and a photographer from the visiting country were both up on ladders next to each other, directly above the visiting dignitary. They began to elbow each other and their ladders were swaying; I could envision one of them falling on top of our honored guest. What an honor that would be.

I raced behind and between them and in a stage whisper I ordered them to stop and get down. Believe it or not, the American photographer in a whiny voice said to me, "He started it." It was like being back in grade school.

On the other hand, I worked occasionally with David Kennerly, Pulitzer Prize–winning photographer, who sent me an incredible picture he took of the Reagans. They are standing facing each other, out on the Truman balcony, with the Washington Monument in the background. They were clearly sharing a special moment talking together. David took the picture from inside the Yellow Oval Room through the windowpanes, which really made it unique; he expected it to be used in *Time* magazine and was surprised when editors rejected it. They said it was "too schmaltzy." David tried to explain that that's the way the Reagans are with each other: schmaltzy. He felt strongly that it was a good relationship picture. I can attest to that.

David said he loved dealing with Nancy. She wasn't "bossy"; he said she was "delightful to work with—helpful, understanding and genuine." And David allowed me to unveil his schmaltzy picture.

David said that Nancy "was right up there with people I really liked."

13

Diplomat in Chief

Nancy Reagan was a natural diplomat. It just took me a while to think of her that way. She was naturally cautious, thoughtful, and soft-spoken. She gave you her undivided attention. All important attributes for a diplomat.

As she became more comfortable and self-assured as First Lady, she built friendly relationships with many members of the press, and with many in the Washington establishment like Kay Graham and Lucky Roosevelt.

When they traveled internationally, she was a valuable asset to President Reagan. She developed strong ties with world leaders and their families, particularly Nouha Alhegelan, wife of the Saudi Arabian ambassador, and Jehan Sadat, the wife of Egypt's president, Anwar Sadat, who mentioned in her own book that Nancy Reagan became one of her best friends in Washington.

Nancy so impressed Chinese leader Deng Xiaoping on a trip to China that he flirted with her, inviting her to return to visit China again, but without President Reagan. Deng later said to President Reagan, "I hear Mrs. Reagan read a lot about China before you left." And turning to Nancy, he said, "You have done a lot for our giant pandas, thank you." He was referring to a campaign we launched in advance of the trip asking kids across the country to collect and send Nancy "Pennies for Pandas." The children's contribution would go toward buying bamboo, which was in short supply. It was a great way to connect our two countries with our mutual love of panda bears.

After Nancy accompanied the president as he called on heads of state in France, Italy, England, and West Germany in 1982, the German magazine *Bunte* featured a four-page article about Nancy Reagan with the headline: "Nancy Reagan— America's Best Diplomat." *Bunte* described Nancy as acting as a hostess for representatives of the American community in front of the Petit Palais in Paris and as diplomatically charming as she sat next to France's president Mitterrand at the American embassy in Paris. She was described as "benefactor" when she visited the National Institute for the Blind in Paris, presenting them with a much needed stereo. More compliments followed: Nancy as opera fan and art lover, visiting Monet's Giverny, proclaiming her love for Monet's work and wishing she could stay forever. And she paid her silent respect as she laid a wreath on the thirty-eighth anniversary of the American invasion of Normandy in 1944. Before leaving she took a tour of Omaha Beach where thousands of Americans lost their lives during the landing. For those of us who accompanied her, it was incredibly moving.

The *Denver Post* ran an amusing story about one incident

on this trip. The reporter says that Hannelore Schmidt, wife of the German chancellor, asked Nancy what she did to keep smiling while posing for the cameras. Nancy told her she always recited the alphabet. So, they stood side by side and posed for the cameras while each whispered the alphabets of their respective languages. That's how Nancy made it fun and made a friend.

That trip created a great deal of goodwill among Europeans. Nancy left a strong impression. She was graceful, attentive, friendly, and above all, she was quite "diplomatic."

* * *

Very early in President Reagan's first term, over Memorial Day weekend in 1981, the White House social secretary Muffie Brandon received a cable from her sister-in-law, Jane Abell Coon, newly appointed ambassador to Bangladesh. President Ziaur Rahman had been assassinated. Ambassador Coon asked if Muffie could arrange for Nancy Reagan to send a note of sympathy and condolences to the president's widow.

Here is Muffie's account:

> I take the cable up to Mrs. Reagan and explain the situation. Without a word, she goes immediately to her desk. She reached for her private stationery and writes four or five beautiful consoling sentences and hands me the letter with tears in her eyes.

Remember, this was a scant two months after her own husband had been shot.

That letter, Muffie recounts, was reprinted on the front pages of the major newspapers throughout Bangladesh, and copies of the newspaper article were pasted to roadside shrines throughout the country.

Nancy was touched to learn about the national reaction and more than a little surprised that she had made such a difference.

As Nancy tirelessly worked to connect with world leaders, only Raisa Gorbachev continued to confound her. In her book, Nancy candidly described Raisa's boorish behavior at official teas and luncheons over the years. Nancy saw Raisa as a committed Marxist who was incapable of repressing her need to dominate every conversation with details on the joys of communist life. I can see why Nancy would have found that behavior difficult to tolerate.

When Nancy lost both her father and later her mother, and when Nancy suffered breast cancer, she was inundated with flowers and letters from around the world. She told me she never heard a word of condolence or compassion from Raisa.

Then, in 1988, Raisa accompanied her husband to New York City where her husband was to address the UN. At tea, Nancy said Raisa talked but did not lecture, even noting that the Soviet Union had not done a good job caring for children by providing workplace child care when they would have been better served staying in their own homes. For reasons unknown, Nancy said the atmosphere at this event was very different. Raisa told Nancy that she and her husband would miss them when they left the White House and would very much like them to visit the Gorbachevs in Moscow.

I asked former secretary of state George Shultz how he viewed the obvious dislike between Raisa and Nancy. He said Raisa was a very difficult woman, which is as strong a negative statement any diplomat would make. He added, "They just never clicked."

* * *

George Shultz was secretary of state from 1982 to 1989. Immediately prior to that he was Treasury secretary.

He was a favorite of Nancy's. He described her as "a terrific person" and he loved talking about her. As secretary of state he was always invited to every White House state dinner, which he referred to as "a real party, great fun for the guests." He said, "Nancy always took care of me at state dinners; I usually sat next to Hollywood starlets." He especially remembers sitting with Ginger Rogers with whom he danced at the end of the evening. He has a framed picture of that dance, which Ginger inscribed: "For a minute I thought I was dancing with Fred. Let's do it again." For the younger generations, Fred Astaire and Ginger Rogers were the two most wonderful dancers and movie stars in days long gone.

He vividly recalls what he feels was Nancy's most famous, and perhaps important, diplomatic moment. Soviet foreign minister Andrei Gromyko said to Nancy, "Does your husband want peace?" To which she immediately responded, "Of course he does."

Gromyko, who was taller than Nancy, leaned down toward her ear and said, "Whisper peace in his ear every night." She pulled him down toward her to respond into his ear, "And I will whisper peace into your ear. Peace."

To my mind, Nancy's greatest diplomatic impact was in South Korea.

We were preparing to depart for Seoul, South Korea, for an official visit late in 1983 when we had a last-minute request from our ambassador there, Richard L. "Dixie" Walker, and his wife that we consider meeting two children in desperate need of open heart surgery. The little boy suffered from a hereditary disease called VSD, ventricular septal defect, and the little girl had ASD, atrial septal defect. South Korean medicine was not yet advanced enough to correct the defects. These children were being "sponsored" by a fledgling organization called Gift of Life started by the Rotary Club in Manhasset, Long Island, New York, in partnership with St. Francis Hospital.

Nancy, a true doctor's daughter, brushed aside staff objections to meeting the children, based on the concern that we would be inundated with other kids needing some kind of help. She met with the families privately in the ambassador's residence and we took those two beautiful children with us on the plane when we returned to the United States: a boy and a girl, aged four and seven, named Lee Kil Woo and Ahn Ji Sook.

The reporters on the plane, just like the staff, fell in love with these two engaging children. Because of their conditions, they turned blue after walking more than a few steps and had to squat down to recover. Once aboard the plane, the little boy became fascinated by one reporter's computer and sat on his lap pretending to type for most of the trip.

After a brief stop at Andrews AFB to unload the travelers, Nancy took the children on to St. Francis Hospital on Long Island where their surgery was scheduled with support from the Gift of Life program. Frank Regnante, the hospital's director of development, had worked with Rotarian Robert Donno to try to find a way to bring the children from Seoul for the surgery. They found a way, thanks to Nancy.

On December 19, 1983, Nancy returned to visit the children in New York after their surgery. Nancy took Cabbage Patch dolls and T-shirts for the kids, and more presents for the other children in the same hospital. The two Korean children presented Nancy with a Christmas tree ornament they had made for her at the St. Francis Hospital Christmas party the day before.

They made Christmas cards as well. Lee's card read: To my "hal maw nee" (grandmother in Korean); Ahn signed hers: "Thank you for saving my life."

Many years later, we discovered, to our surprise, that both children were given up for adoption and ended up as brother and sister in Flagstaff, Arizona. They later moved from Flagstaff with their family to Seattle. Their American names are Brett and Diana Halvorson.

Brett wrote to Nancy in 2007 after reading in the news that she had been hospitalized after a fall. He wanted to thank her for what she had done for him—he credits her with saving his life—and she began corresponding with him, inviting him to visit with her at the Reagan Library, to attend a talk by Tony Snow and then to a small private dinner afterward. In her letter to him after her fall, she said she guessed it was time for her to give up roller skating.

Brett now teaches English as a second language in Seoul and continues to work as a volunteer for the Gift of Life Foundation. He is an incredible example of paying back what you owe, helping to provide access to lifesaving cardiac medical care for children from other developing nations. Now, with real pride, he can bring them to South Korea for their treatment.

Brett told me that Lee Soon-ja, the First Lady of South Korea at that time, started a foundation because of Nancy Reagan's work, to help children and adults with cardiac problems.

Brett's adoptee sister, Diana, is also healthy and happy, living a productive life on the West Coast. I can still see her beautiful seven-year-old face as if it were yesterday.

When I located Brett, he had reunited with his birth family. He says that meeting Nancy and being reunited with his Korean family were the two best days of his life. His birth parents are divorced so he met them separately. He spent the night with his father and awoke in the middle of the night crying, feeling guilty for all he had compared to his biological family. He also met his three younger siblings and the older brother of whom he had retained a fuzzy memory.

When he met his mother, she kept repeating the Korean word for "sorry" and crying and hugging him. Brett said that it might sound silly but that was when he finally felt "whole." I didn't think it was silly at all. I am sure his mother had grieved for him but gave him up to ensure he would get the best medical care available, not just in the hospital but afterward. She and his father had helped save his life as much as the surgeons at St. Francis.

Mr. Donno says that the decision by Nancy Reagan to help two critically ill Korean children changed the trajectory of Gift of Life in "magical ways." In 1975 this Rotarian-based program had begun its mission of bringing one child at a time from developing countries to the United States for cardiac treatment. For Gift of Life, the extraordinary media coverage of these two little children captivated Americans across the country and gave it the impetus to expand its reach and capacity that ultimately led, in 2003, to the creation of Gift of Life International. According to recent reports, the organization has transported over thirty thousand children to the United States for lifesaving surgery.

Many years later, Nancy told me she was stunned by the knowledge that those two wonderful children were alive because she had been in a position to help them.

And to this day I think about the goodwill that gesture generated for generations of South Koreans. I'd call it powerful diplomacy.

14

Planes, Trips, and Weather Reports

Nothing compares to the experience of traveling with the president and his wife to events far and wide.

Hundreds of people are involved in a presidential visit. By contrast, several dozen people support a First Lady trip. We call them "advance" men and women. They are responsible for detailed planning of every moment the president and/or First Lady is in public.

The advance team for Nancy had to work twice as hard as the presidential advance because we didn't have the depth of support that was available to the president. That meant, for example, we needed one member of our advance team to work with the local phone company to set up our communications needs. The president brought his communications system with him. Our visits were lower key, at least when we could have our way.

The president's motorcade had, in our day, as many as fifteen to twenty cars that moved at high speed with sirens blaring. Nancy was escorted around town in a two- or three-car motorcade and we never used a siren. And we stopped for traffic lights. Most people we passed never noticed us.

On one trip, legendary in the annals of the First Lady's advance team, we went to Columbia, South Carolina, in October 1984. Nancy was visiting a fourth-grade class at Rosewood Elementary School to learn about and draw attention to its antidrug program called "I'm special."

The advance team, led by our favorite advance man of all time, Marty Coyne, sat down in a meeting with the chief of police whom Marty described as the salt of the earth, a guy who'd come up through the ranks and was without a doubt "the boss."

Logistics was the topic, how to get Nancy from one place to the next. Marty explained to the chief that Nancy wanted her presence to be low-key. The chief looked at Marty and said, "Young man, when the First Lady is in my city, we don't do anything low-key." And that's how it came to be that we were escorted to and from the school and from and to the airport by twenty-five motorcycle cops.

And back at the airport Nancy stood with each of them to shake twenty-five hands and have individual pictures taken with each of them.

It was a tradition of the Reagans (and also the Bushes after them) to stand plane side on departure and personally thank and have photos taken with every member of the local police force, as well as other volunteers who helped escort them during their trip.

The other complication for us on that trip: the advance

team booked everyone into the Hyatt Hotel. Then Senator Strom Thurmond had his aide call to acquaint our team with the fact that the Marriott was "the Republican hotel." Nobody argued with Strom; we moved to the Marriott.

Another of my favorite Marty Coyne advance stories I'd describe as "colorful" is when Nancy flew to London for the July 23, 1986, wedding of Prince Andrew and "Fergie." The Duke and Duchess of York were to be married at Westminster Abbey.

Marty met with Nancy's chief of staff, Jack Courdamache, when they first arrived and Jack explained there was an issue. The American ambassador's wife was planning to wear a dress and hat in the exact same color to the wedding as the dress and hat Nancy Reagan had brought to wear.

Being a guy, Marty admitted that at first he wasn't sure what the problem was. Once it was explained to him, Marty went to the deputy chief of mission (the number two guy) at the embassy and explained the problem. The DCM was no fool and told Marty he needed to go directly to the ambassador, Charles Price.

Marty gets an appointment with the ambassador at 8:00 a.m. the next day and the ambassador tells him that his wife is not going to change her wardrobe.

Our team came up with a masterful solution. By protocol, Nancy was seated at the front of the church. Normally, the ambassador and his wife would be with her. Instead, they were seated with other ambassadors and wives a good distance behind. Nor was the ambassador's wife ever seen in Nancy's presence. No one—and by this I mean the press because that was all we press secretaries cared about—ever noticed the similarity in attire.

* * *

Ann Wrobleski—a smart-as-a-whip graduate of Stevens College and a veteran congressional aide before joining the East Wing staff as Nancy's projects director—told me a great story about traveling with the First Lady:

> As part of her drug awareness campaign, Nancy accepted an invitation from the Parent Teacher Association (PTA) to speak to its national convention in Las Vegas.
>
> This was before Las Vegas became a "family" destination.
>
> Nancy Reagan, the PTA, and Las Vegas—tailor-made for a late-night comedy monologue. After the visit was announced, I received a call from the senior aide to Senator Paul Laxalt, Nevada's senior senator. He was often referred to as "the First Friend" since he and President Reagan had been friends since their days as western governors together. The purpose of the call was to say that the senator hoped Nancy wouldn't make any Las Vegas jokes during her remarks. The speechwriter would be very disappointed—the best material went down the drain.
>
> Since it was a drug awareness event, I went on what is called the "preadvance" with the Secret Service and a volunteer advance man. Meanwhile, Frank Sinatra had called Nancy and insisted she make use of his apartment at the Sands Hotel.

The agents, the advance man, and I toured Sinatra's apartment. It was full of beautiful antiques and decorated in muted tones. In the bedroom was a large four-poster bed with tasteful bed hangings. This was in sharp contrast to my hotel room, which featured orange shag carpet and a round purple bed.

We also toured the floor of the casino with the managers of the hotel. At one point, they asked if Nancy would want to come to the casino and play the slots. I replied, "Certainly not." They then asked if she might want to play in private; they could move a machine to Sinatra's living room. I mumbled something dismissive and forgot about it.

When we got back to Washington, Nancy wanted to know all about Sinatra's apartment and I described it. She was skeptical.

Just a few days later, the same Laxalt aide called and asked if I knew about a request from the Sands to the Nevada Gaming Commission to move a slot machine to Frank Sinatra's apartment during the visit of the First Lady. He explained he'd been alerted by the commission and that the request would necessarily be made public the next day according to Nevada law.

My life flashed before me—all thirty-two years. I envisioned the *Washington Post* headline "Nancy Plays Slots in Sinatra's Las Vegas Pad" and heaven only knows what the headline writers at the *New York Post* would create.

I assured the Senate aide that this was a misunderstanding and he assured me that he would take care of canceling the request.

When we arrived at Sinatra's apartment, Nancy walked through the living room directly into the bedroom I'd described to her.

And luckily, to my great relief, there was no slot machine in sight.

* * *

I had forgotten (or blocked from memory) how detailed the plans were for every trip until I came upon a number of "trip books," handed out at the start of every trip as we got on the plane at Andrews Air Force Base.

Here is an example of the detailed planning that went into a relatively straightforward First Lady trip to New York City on October 11 and 12, 1983:

- On October 11 we were to meet at the Ad Council offices to review the antidrug ad campaign the Ad Council had asked Needham, Harper & Steers Ad Agency to recommend.
- We were to arrive at the Ad Council's front door at precisely 1:25 p.m. for an initial meeting.
- We were to leave there at 2:45 p.m. to travel to the Carlyle Hotel where we would arrive at 3:00 p.m. to remain overnight.
- On Wednesday, October 12, at 5:50 a.m. we would depart en route to the ABC Studios.
- Ten minutes later we would arrive.
- At 9:15 a.m. we would retrace our steps and return to the hotel.
- In between, Nancy spent an entire two-hour program on *Good Morning America*, which was devoted to her Just Say No campaign.

- Back at the hotel, Nancy goes to a private luncheon with friends, leaving directly from there to LaGuardia and we are all back at the White House at 4:15 p.m.

The trip book provides a TAB A, the seating chart for the meeting at the Ad Council. Mrs. Reagan was seated with a former resident of Phoenix House, the drug treatment center, to her right and the mother of an addicted child to her left. Six representatives for Needham, Harper & Steers were there with their creative recommendations. The president of the Ad Council and the director of the National Institute on Drug Abuse, as well as the vice president of public relations for New York Life, were also there. Just Say No was born, and that trip book was eighty pages long.

During my tenure as Nancy's press secretary I traveled far and wide with the Reagans. Several memories from our travels through China stand out in my mind.

At one point on a China trip we were staying at the Jin Jiang Hotel in Shanghai. Thankfully, only for one night. In 1984, Chinese hotels were not up to the standards of the Western world. I shared a four-bedroom suite with three other women. We quickly discovered we had other guests. Cockroaches. Big cockroaches. As soon as you turned out the light, armies of roaches came marching in. The four of us stayed up most of the night sitting together in the common living room in long robes, towels on our heads, and socks on our feet with the lights on.

The trip came not long after we'd entertained Mr. T at the White House when he played Santa. He gave us a huge pile of Mr. T car air fresheners as a gift. I had brought some of those on the China trip. We hung them all over our rooms at the roach palace, wondering how long it would take our hosts to figure out what the strange hanging items represented. I like to think it boosted Mr. T's ratings in China.

I do know his visit created lots of excitement at the White House mess when several of us took Mr. T, playing Santa Claus, to lunch the day he visited. Word spread quickly that Mr. T was in the mess and Vice President Bush showed up with a White House photographer. That same night I dropped by the vice president's annual Christmas party at his residence on Observatory Circle. There in the foyer for all to see was a framed picture of George H.W. Bush with Mr. T.

One morning during our stay in China, Nancy called me to the Reagans' suite. She handed me a stack of paper and whispered to me, "Please have these burned." I looked down and quickly ascertained what she'd given me. So I whispered back, "Mrs. Reagan, these are just AP wire stories." In other words, news items that had already been circulated worldwide. She replied, "Please, just do it." I accomplished my assignment. I have no idea why.

We also traveled to Xi'an to see the fantastic Terracotta Warriors, first unearthed only ten years earlier. Excavation of this enormous site continues to this day. When we were there, I recall there was a dustup between our team and the Chinese over what airplane the press would take. They insisted we fly China Air and we capitulated. It was a no-frills flight.

Luckily, the president and Nancy were on Air Force One.

At one point during the flight I slipped into the bathroom. As I was washing my hands I noticed a pocket-sized comb sealed in cellophane. It was quite pretty, with a multicolored floral design. It looked so "occidental." I confess it left the restroom in my possession because I thought it would be a neat keepsake for Rusty, the volunteer in our office back at the White House who answered the phones and helped with the mail.

When I got home and gave it to Rusty, she opened it and we read the stamped "Made in the USA" imprint on the back. The Chinese have a great sense of humor.

On a presidential trip to Japan, there was a reception to which the staff was invited. Elaine Crispin, Nancy's personal secretary who later succeeded me in the second term as press secretary, attended with me. There was a formal tea ceremony that was quite impressive—artistic and graceful. As the beautiful woman who conducted the ceremony handed me and Elaine our cups, we leaned down to drink and Elaine whispered to me, "This looks like the bottom of my fish tank." Her timing was less than impeccable because at that precise moment I had taken a sip and instantly spit it out my nose and mouth in reaction to her hilarious comment. So much for ceremony. And so much for our diplomatic graces.

On the other hand, Nancy went to visit a shrine on that trip. As is customary, we all took our shoes off upon arrival. She was going to speak, so the Japanese made sure to have a translator there. When Nancy left the building, she realized her shoes were inside the shrine and she sent Elaine back to get them. The translator came to me to ask if that was Mrs. Reagan who came back to pick up the shoes. I told her no, the person who came back was Mrs. Reagan's personal assistant.

She looked at me, giggled, and said, "You know, you Americans all look alike to us." So I guess everything evened out.

On one of our numerous presidential trips to London, we were staying at the Churchill Hotel. Our press operation on the hotel's first floor was in the midst of being broken down and moved to our next stop. I was paged to call Mrs. Reagan so I went into the cavernous room to find a phone. No one else was in the huge, cavernous room but me.

I found a working phone, got connected, and sat down at a long press table while we talked. A peculiar-looking fellow walked in, came toward me smiling, leaned down, and picked up the tablecloth so he could look under the table. At first I assumed he was there to break down the room and disable that last working phone. But he kept looking up at me and smiling, and then back to looking under the table. I saw no need to alarm Nancy, but I definitely sensed something weird was going on so I started looking for someone to pass by who could help me. Finally, one of our Secret Service agents walked by. I caught his eye and pointed down, all the time talking to Nancy. As the agent walked toward me, my strange visitor took off running, the agent in hot pursuit. Later that day I got a call from Scotland Yard asking me if I wanted to press charges against the gentleman, a known pedophile who liked looking at ladies' feet. I demurred. And I beat feet out of London.

The international trips were memorable, but we did most of our traveling in the good old USA. On one trip to Los Angeles, we stopped in Phoenix as usual so Nancy could spend one night with her mother. I took advantage of the sunny weather and went out to the pool at the Biltmore where I was staying. I was paged and the person on the phone looking for me was Frank Sinatra. You should have seen how the folks lying around the pool looked up when they heard the page. He was calling from Los Angeles about some concern he had with arrangements for a state dinner proposal coming from the White House. But, for one short moment, all eyes were on me!

15

Protecting Nancy

Whenever Nancy left the confines of the White House it was necessary that she travel with security. Her lead agent, George Opfer, held that position for six years. He remembers getting the call from John Simpson, head of the Secret Service, a day or two after the 1980 election telling him he was being assigned to protect Nancy. Off he flew to Los Angeles, where a few days later he found himself meeting Nancy in the Reagans' Pacific Palisades home. Little did he know at the time how this assignment would impact his life.

Until now George has never cooperated in any interviews about Nancy because he felt that to do his job he had to be privy to much of the Reagans' personal life, and that the moments he'd witnessed did not belong to him. Those were my exact feelings about writing a book about Nancy until I realized there was an important story to tell that was missing from history.

George had a good relationship with his "protectee," known

by her code name "Rainbow" to her agents. She trusted him and the other agents completely, although Joe Sullivan used to jokingly complain that whenever he was in the lead position because George had the day off, Nancy would ask, "Where is George?"

When President Reagan was shot, George stayed close by Nancy's side as she waited for word on the surgery. They sat together in the hospital chapel and he handed her his handkerchief.

George reminded me of our trip to Monaco for Princess Grace's funeral. Nancy was to stay at the palace. When she got there, she asked George where he was staying. He said he was staying at a hotel, quite a distance from the palace. She apparently made a few inquiries because George soon found himself with a room at the palace. The idea of having your lead agent several miles away was not Nancy's idea of protection.

At another funeral back in Washington, he sat in his usual position behind her at the service, surveying the room, eyes sweeping from side to side. Unfortunately, neither George nor I are able to remember whose funeral this was. Apparently, Nancy recognized during the service that George was favoring one side over the other and that in that favored direction sat a very attractive young lady. Afterward, Nancy, with obvious amusement, asked George if his neck was stiff. She knew. And loved teasing him. We came to believe Nancy really did have eyes in the back of her head.

Without any encouragement from me, George said he would like people to know that Nancy Reagan was a "real person, a decent, caring human being." He said, "She could spot a phony.... She was a good judge of character." There was emotion in his voice.

He went on to tell me this:

> When it was time for me to be transferred from Mrs. Reagan's detail, I had to meet with the president and Director John Simpson who advised me that I would have to speak to Mrs. Reagan. They were not going to tell her that I was leaving her security. So I met with Mrs. Reagan and she became very emotional about my departure since I'd been with her through all the good and bad days.
>
> She wanted to make sure that the transfer was the best for my career and I was not being forced off her detail. We had numerous conversations but she only wanted what was best for me. She always said I was like a member of her family and she would call me afterwards just to see how I and my family were doing.

While I don't know it for a fact, I suspect Nancy lobbed in a few calls to try to extend George's service on her detail when she learned he was being rotated off in 1986. But the Secret Service has its rules. Not even Nancy Reagan could break through them.

During the Christmas holidays that year, Nancy wrote George this note as he was being reassigned:

> *Dear George—*
> *I can't believe this is the last Christmas we'll be together—in fact I refuse to believe it—like Scarlett, I'll think about it tomorrow.*

Within days of the first Reagan inaugural, we spent a day in the Red Room working with the professionals from *Vogue* shooting a cover photo of Nancy in her inaugural gown. *(Courtesy of the Ronald Reagan Presidential Library)*

Just before the wedding of the century—Prince Charles and Lady Diana—we dined at the American Embassy. I was there with Nancy, Peter McCoy, and Barbara Walters of NBC. *(Courtesy of the Ronald Reagan Presidential Library)*

Nancy met regularly with her staff to plan activities. This photo was taken in the Diplomatic Reception Room during one of those sessions. Chief of staff Peter McCoy, Nancy, and me. We were probably laughing because of a joke Peter told. He had no equal. *(Courtesy of the Ronald Reagan Presidential Library)*

On our first flight of many to a drug treatment center, Nancy stands in the "gaggle" of press who are asking her every question imaginable. That's me nearby with a worried look on my face. *(Courtesy of the Ronald Reagan Presidential Library)*

Whenever the president met with another head of state, Nancy invited the spouse for tea. In this photo, Nancy tries to get a word in edgewise. Raisa Gorbachev, a committed Marxist, tended to dominate every conversation. *(Courtesy of the Ronald Reagan Presidential Library)*

Nancy and Gary Coleman, child star of *Diff'rent Strokes,* enjoy a laugh as they rehearse on a Hollywood set. This appearance was directed at kids and was very effective at educating them about the dangers of drug use. *(Photograph by Larry Rubenstein, Reuters)*

I introduce Santa and friends to President Reagan in the Oval Office. Santa always made an appearance around the holidays. Some people called him Willard Scott, the weatherman at NBC. *(Courtesy of the Ronald Reagan Presidential Library)*

When the Indiana Pacers played the Philadelphia 76ers, they invited Nancy to help them draw attention to the youth drug abuse issue; Nancy took dead aim. Deputy press secretary Betsy Koons Robertson worked out the angles and even stood in as Nancy for a trial run. At the game, Charles Barkley of the 76ers and the Pacers' Wayman Tisdale lifted Nancy up to the basket, and she slam-dunked the ball. The crowd gave her a standing ovation! *(Courtesy of the Ronald Reagan Presidential Library; photographer: Mary Anne Fackelman)*

Nancy and her social secretary Muffie Brandon take a close look at the unveiling of the new Reagan China, while I discuss media coverage with chief of staff Peter McCoy. *(Courtesy of the Ronald Reagan Presidential Library)*

Nancy Reagan changed her image overnight with her surprise appearance on stage at the Gridiron Club. After a year of press criticism, Nancy brought the media elite to their feet for several standing ovations when she showed them her sense of humor and her ability to make fun of herself. Her escort, Charlie McDowell, Washington bureau chief for the *Richmond Times-Dispatch,* was the president of the Gridiron Club. He and Helen Thomas of UPI were the only journalists in on the secret. *(Courtesy of the Ronald Reagan Presidential Library; photographer: Jack Kightlinger)*

Nancy loved babies. She cuddled with them whenever she had the chance. This baby was at a London orphanage where the First Lady visited during one of the president's European tours. *(Courtesy of the Ronald Reagan Presidential Library)*

In 1984, the president and Mrs. Reagan visited China, and Nancy was charmed by these Chinese children dancing and singing. The president charmed the Chinese by working hard to speak a few words in their language. *(Courtesy of the Ronald Reagan Presidential Library)*

Edie Davis, Nancy's mother, and her precious red woolen gloves are surrounded by Patti Davis, President Reagan, and Nancy during a visit to Phoenix where Mrs. Davis lived. Mrs. Davis, suffering from dementia, found great comfort in those gloves. Nancy treasured those red woolen gloves until she died. *(Courtesy of the Ronald Reagan Presidential Library; photographer: Mary Anne Fackelman)*

Amie Garrison was a five-year-old in desperate need of a liver. Amie, with very little time left to live, is introduced by Nancy to a very surprised press corps, who were only expecting to preview the White House Christmas decorations. The press corps rose to the occasion and were instrumental in getting out the word that Amie's family was desperate to locate a liver match. Thanks to the team of Nancy Reagan and Tom Starzl, pioneering transplant surgeon from the University of Pittsburgh Medical Center, this story had a happy ending. *(Courtesy of the Ronald Reagan Presidential Library)*

The Pulitzer Prize–winning photographer David Hume Kennerly was very surprised when *Time* took a pass on this picture. The editor at *Time* told David it was too schmaltzy. David tried to explain that the Reagans were genuinely schmaltzy. Lucky for this author because I get to unveil this wonderful picture for the first time. David took it standing inside the White House residence while the Reagans stood outside on the balcony. The geometric lines created by the windowpanes and the Washington Monument make the picture especially interesting. *(Courtesy of Dave Hume Kennerly)*

I'll miss you terribly as you know but there are lots of memories—as you said, some were peaks, some valleys. And they all stand out vividly in my mind. From the day we sat in the hospital and after handing me your handkerchief you said "all we can do now is pray"—and that began everything—I've depended on you so much for so many things. There's going to be a large void in my life but I'm trying to be a big girl about it and if this is what you want and it will be good for you—okay—but I don't like it!

There are so many things I have to thank you for—and I do—but if I stop to think about them you'll have to give me your handkerchief again—

Bless you and Merry Christmas,
Rainbow

This was in reference to a note she sent him shortly after the assassination attempt where she wrote: "Thank you, George, as always, for coming to my rescue—here it is back all cleaned and pressed." It ended with a smiley face. The handkerchief was enclosed.

George also shared with me the beautiful note Nancy sent him dated January 29, 1989. In that note, she wrote about his presence when she arrived in Washington, and then at the helicopter to see her and President Reagan off to California when they left office. She wanted him to remember that he was with her through the good and the bad times.

After he retired from the Secret Service, George stayed in touch with Nancy mainly by telephone. He also visited her at her residence over the years and sometimes they would go out for lunch. I can picture Rainbow and George sitting in the dining room of the Bel-Air Hotel reminiscing about all the old times. I bet they gossiped a bit. And maybe even laughed about how Secret Service director Simpson and President Reagan refused to be the ones to break the bad news to Nancy when George was being transferred.

George sent me an email saying he believes Nancy and President Reagan would be honored by my book. I think she'd be most pleased that he made known his devotion to "Rainbow."

* * *

I do not remember a single agent assigned to the First Lady's detail who didn't become part of our extended East Wing family.

Because I was frequently on television in my role as press secretary, I learned quickly the danger associated with that chore. One very disturbed man kept showing up at my home in the belief that I could get him a job on the National Security Council. How bizarre is that? He'd seen me on television. The Secret Service alerted the local police to the problem and they drove by frequently to check things out. My children were terrified of him. My husband was so concerned he insisted on sleeping with a weapon at his bedside. Late one evening I turned into our street to see at least six police cars with lights flashing in front of my house. They had received a call from a neighbor about this fellow and knew I was his target; they had him down on the ground when I pulled into my driveway. The Fairfax County, Virginia, legal apparatus took over and the last I heard he was being held for mental observation, for which I am truly grateful.

Shortly after the March 30, 1981, assassination attempt, when I had been on TV during the press conference after the president's surgery, a real sicko from Little Rock, Arkansas, began calling and demanding to speak with me, saying he'd seen me on television. He even sent flowers. Betsy, our executive assistant, was being driven to distraction. He called one day and said, "I am in the East Wing and on my way up." That concerned me a lot and I called the Secret Service to report this. They fanned out all over the White House and the grounds and then came to see me, asking me to tell them the whole story. We told them the name he used and mentioned the flowers. Joe Sullivan asked if we knew where the flowers came from and as luck would have it, we had the card that came with the flowers. The Secret Service traced them back to the sender.

Several weeks later, Joe came to see me to tell me that they had just had a visit with this fellow, a "happily married man" by the way, who would not be bothering me again.

It was one of the few times Joe was wrong. Several years later Nancy traveled to Little Rock for an event, which was publicized in advance. Once our team arrived at the hotel, we happened to change the rooms assigned to us to create a more logical arrangement. Fortunately, the hotel records still had me in the original room. That same sick man spent the night calling the original room number, asking for me. How creepy is that?

16

Up Close and Personal

On one early morning flight, I sat across from Nancy and she noticed I was watching her eat her breakfast. So, logically, she asked why I was staring.

I explained that the latest story circulating informally through the press corps was that the reason Nancy stayed so thin was that she chewed every bite of food thirty-two times before swallowing. She laughed heartily.

I went on to say that I was sorry to note it was not true, because I had been counting and had hoped this was the secret to staying fit so I could start to practice it.

Nancy once told me a highly amusing story involving a meeting she had with a woman she invited to the residence for some reason or other. At any rate, they had never met before; Nancy was casually dressed in a blouse and wraparound skirt. As she stood to bid her guest goodbye, Nancy's skirt fell to the floor. She was standing in her slip. She knew her guest was too embarrassed to move; Nancy just giggled as she picked up her skirt and put it back on. She said something to her guest to the effect that this was a meeting she was sure her guest would always remember.

Nancy had meaningful and greatly appreciated advice from former First Ladies. She was particularly fond of Jackie Kennedy whom she regarded as a superb First Lady, especially at such a young age. Nancy told me that Mrs. Kennedy had been very helpful when the Reagans first moved into the White House.

So, naturally, when Bill Clinton was elected in the 1992 election, Nancy reached out to Hillary, writing her a personal note and offering to give her the benefit of her experience, to help the new First Lady in any way she could.

Nancy told me that Hillary never even responded. Nancy said she had absolutely no use for her after that.

Laura Bush was an entirely different story. She graciously invited Nancy to lunch at the White House on May 2, 2005, when Nancy was planning to be in town.

Laura asked Nancy to put together a guest list of ladies she'd like Laura to invite. It was a wonderful reunion. Gahl Burt was there along with Carol Laxalt, Robin Paisley, and Gayle Wilson, among others. I had both Laura and Nancy sign my menu card, something I'd never done before but for some reason this felt historic. I know how much that luncheon meant to Nancy. Seeing her there as a guest was special. And in case you don't already know it, Laura Bush is a sweetheart. Nancy truly loved her.

* * *

You can really learn a lot about someone by how they treat people who work with them. I talked to both Charlie Palmer and Howie Franklin, both former chief stewards aboard Air Force One. They attended to every personal need of the president and First Lady aboard the plane. I wanted to know about their experiences with the Reagans. No one was in a better position to know the Reagans up close and personal.

Both of the Reagans, according to Howie, were very easy to work for. They stuck to their schedules and were always on time; they were infrequent fliers and always very considerate of the crew. Both men said the Reagans were "extremely gracious and polite." Howie mentioned that he admired how Nancy always "dressed beautifully." He also said she was obviously deeply in love with her husband. "They flirted with each other," he said, "and they sure weren't doing it to impress me."

Nancy knew Charlie best, and everyone I spoke to agrees she was really fond of him.

The crew of AF One was invited to the Reagan Library for the dedication of the newly retired plane in the specially built glass pavilion attached to the library. Howie said they were thrilled to sit up front at the ceremony and next to Charlton Heston at that.

Afterward, Nancy walked into the newly installed plane and went all the way to the back until she found Charlie who got a great big hug; she talked to him with tears in her eyes.

Howie told a story about when Nancy and the president were on that very plane. He recounts this story in his own book but he also told it to me personally. They had a refueling stop in Alaska. The president was to leave the plane to greet the people waiting to welcome him. He asked Howie for his trench coat but Nancy objected and kept insisting he wear a different warmer coat with a fur collar. The president argued that he thought he would be overdressed. Nancy did not agree. Howie stood there with both coats during the standoff. The president finally looked at Howie with a resigned look and asked him to give him the fur-collared coat. As he was leaving the cabin he leaned in and quietly said to Howie, "But I'm not wearing my gloves."

Howie said to me, "It was such a guy thing."

The first thing that popped into Charlie's mind when I asked about his remembrances of Nancy was that she always seemed worried about being cold. All of us who worked with her can confirm the veracity of that observation. She'd ask him about their destination with this question, "Am I going to be warm enough?" It was a question we all were asked at some point; eventually we learned to have an answer ready.

* * *

Jane Erkenbeck found herself promoted to special assistant to the First Lady in 1985 after working in several earlier White House positions. In this position, she was Nancy's trusted personal assistant. She handled all her personal needs and was the "messenger" who carried paperwork needing Nancy's attention to her several times a day upstairs in the private residence. She especially looked forward to the last "run" because she was often there when the president came home, and he included her in conversations.

She frequently traveled with Nancy when she went to

New York or Los Angeles. On Jane's first trip with Nancy to New York, shortly after Jane began working for her, Nancy asked Jane to bring two seamstresses who worked for Adolfo up to Nancy's room from the hotel lobby. When she brought the ladies into the room, Nancy sat down on the floor in her bathrobe and asked Jane to walk over next to her. She then proceeded to show the seamstresses the length of Jane's dress and worked with them (all three of them down on the floor) to settle on the desired length. Nancy pointed out to Jane that she'd noticed that all Jane's outfits were a bit too long and since she had nice legs she should show them off.

Jane said she was amazed that the First Lady, with whom she had only recently started working, had gotten down on the floor to help figure out Jane's wardrobe details. Not a side of Nancy that most Americans ever got to see. So, when back in DC, Jane proceeded to have each of her outfits shortened to the right length as frequently as her budget would allow.

Jane also reminded me how Nancy always complained about not sleeping well. Jane told me about a trip to Los Angeles when she woke up at 5:14 a.m. to a hotel room that was rocking and shaking. She ran across the hall and checked with the Secret Service Command Post to confirm they'd just experienced an earthquake.

"I had been asked to wake Nancy at 8:30 a.m. and wondered if I should check on her at 5:14 a.m. I finally decided to wait to see if Nancy called my room."

All was quiet. At 8:30 a.m., Jane went into Nancy's room and awakened her. Jane asked her if she'd been disturbed by the earthquake. Nancy replied, "What earthquake?" So much for not sleeping well.

Jane laughed as she reminisced about Nancy's total absence of culinary expertise. One night in LA, Nancy made arrangements for Ron and his wife, Doria, to join her for dinner in her hotel room. Her son and his wife were known for never being on time.

Jane went into Nancy's suite and asked if she needed any help preparing because she, Jane, was going out to dinner with friends. Nancy said no; she said she was going to eat right away and was keeping Ron's and Doria's meals in the warming oven. Before she left, Jane went into the kitchen and discovered the meals were, in fact, in the warming oven but Nancy had failed to turn it on. They both had a good laugh.

* * *

As Nancy declined during the years after President Reagan's death, her friends circled around and tried to keep her spirits up. She suffered from glaucoma as well the lingering effects of a broken pelvis. Both afflictions made getting out and around very difficult and ultimately impossible. I can still picture her walking down the hall in her home—I was visiting from the East Coast—and she had to hold on to the wall to steady herself.

Jane remained a lifelong friend of Nancy's, and sometimes she and one of her daughters would take her out for lunch. When going out became too difficult, Nancy would invite her friends to come for lunch or tea at her home. Jane especially remembered one visit when her daughter kept breaking up cookies and giving them to Nancy. Nancy always loved cookies.

Nancy sent Jane into her bedroom to see a newly acquired picture of Nancy's mother hanging on her wall. The picture was of her mother in her sixties or seventies and Nancy loved it. She especially loved that the picture had belonged to a family friend of Edie's. When the friend passed away, her daughter did some detective work, found out the identity of the person in the portrait, got in touch, and send the picture to Nancy. Jane said Nancy said, "She could have sold it on eBay and made money but instead she gave it to me." Nancy was the kind of person who was loyal to her friends and always touched by the kindness of a stranger. This was a typical example.

17

Blame It on Nancy

I took a call one morning from a reporter inquiring about a rumor that Nancy had canceled a sumo wrestling match scheduled in the Rose Garden after she learned about it. Seemed like a strange story but I called Nancy anyway to check on it. She sighed and said she'd never even heard of any sumo wrestling event let alone canceled it. She added, "Sometimes I feel like if it's raining, it must be my fault."

In truth, the First Lady—any First Lady—provides a convenient excuse for staff on occasion for doing or not doing something. Everyone who has worked in the White House knows that is true.

Once, a few days before President Reagan was to hold a prime-time news conference in the East Room, the chief usher called Mark Weinberg, assistant White House press secretary to President Reagan, to say that Mrs. Reagan did not want the TV production truck to be parked on the north driveway of the White House. He claimed the First Lady did not think it looked very good to have it there and wanted it moved to somewhere much less visible.

Mark was suspicious. He found it hard to believe because he knew Nancy well enough to know she didn't involve herself in anything as insignificant as this. But since the chief usher was in close contact with her, Mark couldn't dismiss the possibility. So he decided to call Nancy to confirm but only after he first asked the network producer if the current location was flexible. For a variety of reasons that benefited the White House as much as the network, that truck had to stay exactly where it was, as it had for decades during live press conferences.

Mark called Nancy to discuss the situation. He told her he had been told she did not want the production truck on the north driveway but that people often invoked her name without her knowledge in order to get their way so he felt compelled to double-check. She told him in no uncertain terms that this was the first she had heard of anything to do with a production truck; she had no opinion of where it should be and she did not appreciate her name being used this way. She hoped no one in the press corps was blaming her. Mark reassured her that was not the case and that he would handle things from there. Mark then called the chief usher and told him he had spoken with the First Lady and she had no objection to the truck's location and that consequently it would remain where it always was during live press conferences.

The chief usher had a two-word response: "I see."

* * *

Speechwriter Landon Parvin had left the White House employ after a few years for more gainful private employment but was called back frequently to write important speeches for both the president and for Nancy. He was one of very few speech-writers who could write a serious policy speech, an emotional speech, and a comedic one, each one effective for the various occasions. He was asked to return to write President Reagan's 1987 speech on the growing AIDS epidemic for a fund-raising dinner to benefit AMFAR, the powerful group that was committed to AIDS research. Coincidentally, since I had also left the White House in 1985, I had been retained to handle communications for the event at the Potomac restaurant at The Watergate Hotel. Elizabeth Taylor was chairing the dinner; the room at the restaurant had to be expanded with a large tent extending across the patio to accommodate the huge and growing guest list. Nancy cared that this evening go well; she knew Landon could work through the politics and write a powerful speech. He did not disappoint.

There was great division in the West Wing about how to handle this issue. The very conservative policy shop at the White House had to sign off on the substance. Landon fore-warned Nancy that he expected problems with some of his language since this was a major speech that would be ana-lyzed to death; Landon told her it might very well be necessary for him to invoke her name. She understood. The use of Nancy's name in a policy dispute was very effective. When-ever the bureaucratic infighting got too heated on the AIDS speech, Nancy's name was invoked as "wanting it this way." She had come to realize that sometimes she would be blamed for things she knew nothing about but, in this case, she really did "want it that way."

Landon also discovered that the president had never met

personally with his surgeon general, C. Everett Koop, to discuss the issue of AIDS. That meeting was promptly scheduled so that the surgeon general could brief the president and help him understand the medical implications of the disease and what kind of government support was needed for research and treatment.

Landon recalls the emotional give-and-take on the contents of that speech. Using the First Lady's name when absolutely necessary, Landon says they were able to include language that got the president on the record saying that AIDS couldn't be caught by casual transmission in swimming pools or by drinking water from a public fountain.

Biographer Lou Cannon said that if the president had said this a few years earlier it would have been seen as forward-looking. Landon believes that if not for Nancy, the speech— the result of compromise and occasional invocation of Nancy's name at crucial points—probably would have been seen as a step backward.

The press tended to believe that Nancy was an ultraconservative who pushed her husband in the same direction. It was never true. Nancy's politics, in truth, were based broadly on what was good for her husband. On any number of occasions, I watched senior White House officials blanch at the prospect of having to explain something to Nancy. They sensed that her extraordinarily close relationship with her husband made her very influential. Those of us who worked closely with her were often amused by the macho guys who turned into quivering jelly when meeting with her.

Years later, when I took the better part of a year off from

the private sector to work for George H.W. Bush as his 1988 campaign press secretary, I was present when Barbara said to him, "George, your staff is afraid of me." To which he replied, "Good, keep it that way." He knew that was just fine. Personally, I loved Barbara Bush. She was always a breath of fresh air with an incredible sense of humor.

Later, I confess, I stooped to the practice of invoking a First Lady's name and blamed Barbara Bush for something she knew nothing about—and worse, I knew she knew nothing about it.

During the Gulf War, Saudi prince Khalid bin Sultan was cocommander with General Norman Schwarzkopf. The prince wrote a book, *Desert Warrior*, about his experience and I was retained to assist in publicizing the book in the United States. The prince had never met the former president, and the president was genuinely thrilled to invite him to Kennebunkport. The prince asked my advice on appropriate gifts. I steered him away from the suggestion that he present the former president with an AK-47 from the Highway of Death. Sounded morbid and gruesome to me. I said that was not a good idea because Mrs. Bush did not like guns. I simply made that up—blame it on Barbara. So, instead, the prince presented President Bush with a beautiful, personalized fishing rod and reel.

The prince departed Kennebunkport after a full day of boating and fishing with the former president. President Bush took several staff and me out to dinner. I regaled the table with the story of the AK-47 and President Bush immediately asked if I could still get one for him. For his library. Long story short, I had to become a registered arms dealer; I had my own ATF agent assigned to me. To be of value to the library, the weapon had to be in working order. It was not legal to import an AK-47 in working order except under strict conditions and for historical purposes. Eventually the weapon made land at the Port of Galveston, Texas, where it was personally claimed by the curator of the Bush Library who waited on the docks for its arrival. All because I had blamed Barbara, completely unfairly, as a convenient way to say no.

So, if you get a chance to visit the George H.W. Bush Presidential Library & Museum in College Station, Texas, perhaps you will get to see my personal AK-47 on display. If not, demand it!

18

No Better Friend

Nancy Reagan had the most amazing address book. It was red leather, and it literally bulged with notes. It was formidable. Every phone number she ever wanted was in there.

She knew how to keep in touch. Her circle of friends widened through her White House years, but she never left any of her West Coast friends behind.

They were reluctant to call her, assuming she would be in the middle of some important meeting or event. As often as she reassured them, they hesitated to call. So she became the caller. She wanted to hear familiar voices and learn the details of their daily lives. Afternoons at the ranch were a good time to call. The president would be out chopping wood or clearing trails with Dennis LeBlanc and Barney Barnett. It was quiet.

She called me occasionally, especially after they moved back to California. Her California friends now felt comfortable ringing her up; now she wanted to be sure not to lose touch with her Washington friends. Sometimes her calls came at really inconvenient times, like during my workday when I was billing by the hour, but I always took them. And, truth to tell, we gossiped.

Vice President Bush used to save up jokes for his weekly lunches with President Reagan because he knew how much President Reagan enjoyed a good joke. I used to save up stories for Nancy's calls. Her calls inevitably lasted an hour so there was a lot of saving up to do. She wanted the latest Washington gossip; news about the family, your job, any plans to travel west.

Occasionally she had sad news to convey. It was the time in life when your friends' health deteriorates. Sometimes she needed advice or help with some request she'd received. If she was coming to DC, she wanted to make sure you were going to be at the event.

When my husband, Bill Tate, died suddenly of a heart attack at age fifty-seven, in 1998, she called me weekly and forced me to talk about it. So I would sit in my office with the door closed and cry to her soothing voice on the phone. She said her father had told her that grieving people really do want to talk; they are just embarrassed because they cry so much, so friends shy away from the subject because they don't want you to cry.

Ever since then I follow her example and encourage my friends to talk and cry. Ultimately, they begin to smile again and recall great times and funny stories.

One time she called me to find out if I was coming to the November 9, 2007, opening of a new exhibit at the Reagan Library. I could tell she really wanted me to come. The exhibit was entitled: Nancy Reagan—A First Lady's Style. For some reason I had not received my invitation and did not know about the event.

So my husband and I—I had remarried in 2005—hurriedly made plans to fly to California for the opening. We were walking through the exhibit when I realized why she was so intent on my being there. Up on the wall was painted a quote from me about how a First Lady learns to take the media spotlight that shone on her and turn it around to focus on an important cause. I turned around to see her standing there smiling at me. She was honoring me with that place on the wall, and it felt like someone had just given me one million dollars.

* * *

Chris Wallace, one of the top newsmen in Washington, loved Nancy Reagan. It had its start in the 1940s when Mike Wallace, his dad, was in radio in Chicago. Mike enjoyed having Edie Davis, Nancy's mother, on his show because she was funny, salty, and had a bit of a potty mouth. Years later, when Mike was covering Ronald Reagan when he was governor of California, he was surprised and pleased to find that Ronald Reagan had married Nancy Davis, Edie's daughter, and they resumed a friendship.

Chris first met Nancy in 1980 when he covered Reagan in the general election. His dad called Nancy and made the introductions, and they became friends.

Chris recounted a story told to him by Stu Spencer, the president's longtime political consultant. Stu sent Ed Rollins to talk to Nancy because she had received calls from friends in LA in 1984 complaining that there were no Reagan lawn signs evident anywhere. Rollins was our campaign manager. Stu told Rollins as he left for the meeting, "Don't let her roll you. We are twenty points up."

When Rollins came back from the meeting, Stu took one look at him and said, "She rolled you." Signs went up all over Los Angeles. I love that story.

In 1985 Chris got Nancy to agree to sit for a documentary. He interviewed her at the ranch, at Camp David, and in the White House private residence. Chris said the hardest person to work with on the documentary he was doing on Nancy was Frank Sinatra. Sinatra insisted that whatever he said could not be edited; it would have to be aired in its entirety. NBC explained that was not possible because he could end up talking for three or four minutes—a lifetime in television—and they would not be able to shorten it. Sinatra was not included in the documentary. He was his own worst enemy.

Chris found himself involved in one of the most scandalous personal issues during the presidency. He ran into Nancy Reynolds, a close friend of Nancy's, outside the White House in mid-February 1987. She told him she had just left the First Lady in the residence and that Don Regan had just hung up on Nancy. Nancy Reynolds was shocked.

Chris repeated the information on the news that night. He later learned that the Reagans were sitting in President Reagan's study watching TV that same night while having dinner and they watched his broadcast. The president asked Nancy if Chris's story was true. It was how he learned about his chief of staff's behavior.

Chris also recalled 1987 as the year of the "Deep Freeze." Nancy was very upset with Chris's coverage of the shape of the Reagan presidency, which he described as in deep trouble dealing with Iran Contra, among other issues. The president and Nancy watched Chris's report just before guests arrived for the president's birthday dinner. The president was unhappy and Nancy blamed Chris. She didn't speak to him for a year.

They made up after she was back in Los Angeles. In 1994 he took three of his four children out to Los Angeles and they all visited Nancy. The president was at the ranch. Chris still remembers his seven-year-old jumping on their bed. He and Nancy had a long talk.

When later that year the president's letter about his Alzheimer's was released, Chris called the Reagan home, expecting to leave a message. Nancy picked up the phone and they talked for half an hour. She was vulnerable and open, telling him how much she had hoped these would be the golden years and now he would be robbed of all those memories.

Above all else, Chris describes her as an attentive friend. "She was the most fun, the best company to be with. She was never looking over her shoulder searching for someone more important to talk with. All her attention was on you."

* * *

George Will met Nancy Reagan before the first presidential debate. The Reagans were staying at Wexford, the Virginia estate Jackie Kennedy made famous when she used it as a place to ride. George said he was hunched over a typewriter when Nancy walked by, ruffled his hair, and said, "I see we've got the varsity here." Their friendship developed from that point forward. Nancy found him to be an honest person whose opinions she came to value greatly.

Over the next eight years, the Reagans came to dinner at the Will residence six times. But who's counting?

George and Nancy periodically went to lunch around town. And once they lunched at the historic home of George Mason down near the Bull Run battlefield.

Sometimes, George told me, the lunches were purely social in nature and occasionally she was worried about something or someone. She liked to chat about DC and enjoyed the local gossip.

So what does George remember most about those lunches? "How little she ate. She'd eat a grape." I am quite certain he was exaggerating. At least a little bit.

The Wills were invited to an early state dinner; George was seated at the president's table. That was normally a great honor, but in this case he said some businessman monopolized the conversation, gushing over the president the entire evening and leaving no opportunity for anyone else at the table to enjoy the president's company.

After that, he turned down repeated state dinner invitations until Nancy finally called him and personally asked him if he wanted to come to the Gorbachev dinner where seats were in great demand. "No," he replied, "I hate those dinners." Nancy knew how to break down George's resistance. She said, "I'll seat you next to Joe DiMaggio." George responded immediately, "What time should I be there?" As anyone who knows George is well aware, George Will is an avid baseball fan.

When asked what else he remembers about Nancy, he immediately replied, "She had a great laugh. Throaty. And she was capable of being high spirited and worried at the same time."

* * *

Doug Wick describes himself as a "lefty" Democrat who was "nuts about Nancy." As the son of Reagan friends Mary Jane and Charlie Wick, Doug spent every Christmas Eve of his childhood with the Reagan family. And, during the Reagans' eight years in Washington, every Christmas Day as well. At those celebrations Charles Wick would often play the piano as Nancy sang. And every year someone was dressed up as Santa Claus, including both President and Mrs. Reagan.

According to Doug, Nancy loved matchmaking. He remembers when he brought his girlfriend, Lucy Fisher, home for Christmas. Nancy spent half an hour talking to her away from everyone else. Doug explained that Lucy was a "lefty Harvard girl." Nancy pulled Doug aside after her conversation with Lucy and said, "Don't blow this." He thought Nancy had X-ray vision for good character. "She dogged me to marry Lucy and she turned out to be right."

At Doug and Lucy's wedding, Nancy won over the entire crowd, many of whom were Democrats. A very successful lesbian writer went to Nancy's table and asked her to dance. Without missing a beat, Nancy said, "You lead." And off they went to the dance floor. As usual, Doug says, Nancy was fun and graceful.

He explained that the best testament to how close they

were to Nancy was that more than thirty years ago when he was racing pregnant Lucy to the hospital, Nancy got his second call right after his mother, Mary Jane Wick.

Later, back in private life in Los Angeles, Nancy was upset to learn that Doug's then eight-year-old daughter had been diagnosed with diabetes; he turned to Nancy for help. Nancy appeared at a *Stuart Little* movie premiere with Doug and worked the red carpet to talk about diabetes and stem cell research. Doug had introduced Nancy to the issues surrounding stem cell research, which he believed held the promise of an eventual cure for diabetes. Nancy became a strong advocate.

In addition, he also introduced her to pediatric AIDS activist Elizabeth Glaser who had coffee with the Reagans and talked about pediatric AIDS and the entire HIV landscape. Within a week, President Reagan got involved, helping Doug any way he could to get these issues wide attention.

Later, as Nancy's health began to deteriorate, Doug visited and they talked quite a bit. "Even when she was failing, about two weeks before she died, she still had that kind of girlish flirtation; she was playful."

He said they reminisced about all their Christmases together. Three days before she died, as they talked about the old days, he noticed the book of love letters the president had written to her and he began reading them to her. She began to give him some romantic advice. She told him that a lustrous love relationship had a limited amount of sparkle—that every relationship is like a star. If you knock away any of that sparkle, it doesn't come back. She told him that words spoken in anger can never be unspoken.

* * *

Tessa Taylor is the daughter of legendary leading man Robert Taylor and his wife, German actress Ursula Thiess. The Reagans and Taylors were the closest of friends during the Hollywood years and while raising their young families in the Pacific Palisades and Brentwood, California. They were such good friends that when Robert Taylor died, then governor Ronald Reagan delivered the eulogy at his funeral.

Tessa shared these memories about Nancy:

I knew Uncle Ronnie and Aunt Nancy as a kid, but it was when I was an adult that I really formed a close relationship with Nancy, and she was amazing. She truly became my godmother then. My mother had dementia and a very deep depression and was not communicating well with me. Aunt Nancy was the first person I called for help. She was able to bridge the communications gap. She helped me through the last years of my mom's life. Aunt Nancy would visit Mom in her home for years and then when she was in an assisted living facility; she would just sit with her for hours and reminisce. The old memories were the most vivid and happy.

Aunt Nancy knew I was lonely after mom died, especially during the holidays. She always invited me to Christmas dinner at her home. Patti and Ron and Doria were very sweet to me, too.

Christmas with Aunt Nancy was wonderful, very traditional. She invited lots of friends like David Jones,

the wonderful Los Angeles florist and one of her closest friends; and usually Dennis Revell and Cyndy and,
of course, Patti were there. Dinner was beautifully
prepared—turkey—and always a yule log cake dessert.
And there was a fire going in the dining room for added
coziness.

The Reagan house was always perfect. But always
comfortable. A wonderful homey atmosphere.

I loved those Christmases. I moved north to Washington State four years ago. I visited her before I left and she
told me that Uncle Ronnie would visit her at night. She
took great comfort in those visits. I could tell she was
ready to be with him.

Aunt Nancy had a big soul. I miss her laugh. And her
perfume. (She wore tuberose.)

And like so many others have said, I miss her voice.

* * *

Paul Costello, former assistant press secretary to Rosalynn
Carter in the White House, and campaign press secretary to
Kitty Dukakis when her husband ran against George H.W.
Bush, tells some great Nancy Reagan stories. Sounds unlikely?
Not if you knew Nancy or, for that matter, if you knew Paul.

Paul worked at the Washington office of the Edelman public relations firm with Mike Deaver. He told Mike that while
flying back from the West Coast he read the *Newsweek* article
by Eleanor Clift (October 1, 1995) entitled "The Long Goodbye." It was about the pain of President Reagan's struggle with
Alzheimer's and Nancy's efforts to reunite their family. Paul

told Mike he was touched by it, especially since it appeared at the same time Paul's father was suffering from dementia brought on by Parkinson's disease. Mike suggested that Paul write her a note and tell her exactly what he'd just told Mike.

"Mike convinced me to write Mrs. Reagan, but I knew I couldn't whitewash some negative feelings I had about the Reagans which still lingered from the 1980 campaign loss. So I started out the note honestly," Paul told me. He said, "I am probably the last person in the world to write to you . . ."

Just a few days later, Mike walked into Paul's office, closed the door, and said, "Nancy just called me and she was sobbing reading your letter." In that note, Paul told me, "I tried to convey the pain I felt watching a loved one mentally diminish so rapidly and I wished her the best in uniting her family."

On his next trip to California, again at Mike's urging, Paul took Nancy out to lunch at, of course, the Bel-Air Hotel. "I brought her a copy of *Angela's Ashes*; we had a wonderful two-hour lunch. A lot of laughs. She was great fun. I was totally surprised," he said. I suspect, knowing both Nancy and Paul, Mike knew they would connect.

Days later, Mike said Nancy called him, said how much she enjoyed the lunch. She thought, perhaps, she might have been too open about personal things like her rocky relationship with her children. Paul said he remembered telling Nancy how he, as a parent of young children, learned to forgive his own parents for any transgressions. "I felt much more empathy for my own parents when I had kids, knowing you make a lot of mistakes along the way." She agreed and thought perhaps he had a point.

Some months later, Mike, his wife, Carolyn, and Paul had dinner with Nancy on a return visit to Los Angeles. It was an evening of a lot of laughs and reminiscing about life in the Washington bubble. "I remember I was sitting there thinking about how life changes," Paul said. "Here I was sitting with Mrs. Reagan, having given up some hard-core political hostilities and laughing uproariously at jokes we all shared. Never in my life would I have imagined Nancy Reagan might be a friend." Paul and Nancy kept up a written correspondence for a number of years.

As we talked about Nancy, Paul shared his observation that many of our modern First Ladies were substantial women, especially behind the scenes. His list included Rosalynn Carter whom he said was very instrumental, behind the scenes, in pivotal moments during the Camp David Summit when President Carter, Menachem Begin, and Anwar Sadat met to hammer out Mideast peace. After getting to know Nancy, he included her in his list.

He also told me he recalled that Nancy had sent Kitty Dukakis a note when Mrs. Dukakis revealed her dependence on prescription drugs. Sounds like something Nancy would do.

* * *

Bob Tuttle says that ever since he can remember, the Reagans were part of his life, an important part. "My dad opened his first car dealership in the late 1950s—a Ford dealership—near Hollywood and he sold one of those Fords to Ronald Reagan. That was the beginning of their friendship."

His dad became one of the earliest members of the famous

kitchen cabinet that formed in 1965 to back the unlikely candidacy of a movie actor for governor of California. "From that time to twenty years later when I headed Presidential Personnel at the White House, I was struck by how close the Reagans were to each other and how much they were truly a couple. It was always the 'Reagans' plural, never just him.

"Nancy had a protective streak; she was always making sure her husband's interests came first. And as welcoming as they both were to new friends joining their circle, Nancy had an almost uncanny sense of knowing pretty quickly if someone was there for Ronnie or out for him/herself. And her instincts were often right."

Bob told me things that others echoed: "Whatever you told Nancy stayed with her. She never violated a confidence. Ever. And she had the best sense of humor. She loved to laugh."

Bob said that when he came on board as director of Presidential Personnel, "I heard from Nancy occasionally; her interests were mainly about several specific ambassadorial appointments, appointments to a few boards. When Nancy was interested in a personnel issue, she was very focused. Like other longtime friends of the Reagans, I saw that she had a very good sense of people and their agendas, but interestingly enough, she never tried to run the show in spite of widespread media reports to the contrary."

19

White House Humor

No one loved a joke more than Ronald Reagan did. Vice President George H.W. Bush had a weekly lunch with President Reagan and he always arrived armed with a good joke. Frequently he had to stop by a number of staff offices on his way to lunch in order to get some new jokes before he met the president. He would also preview some of the newly collected jokes on staffers—a trial run of sorts. When I was the previewer for those jokes, I rated it as fifth-grade boys' humor.

How can you not love humor when you work with Ronald Reagan? As he was being wheeled into the operating room at GW Hospital to have a bullet removed from his lung, he looked up and saw his wife for the first time and said, "Honey, I forgot to duck."

I have a copy of the White House transcript of the press briefing after the March 30, 1981, assassination attempt. We were all in various stages of shock. And yet, right there, is Dr. O'Leary's answer to a reporter's question:

Q: You said that the president was conscious for much of the time. What, if anything, did he say?

A: Well, the surgeons said that his last remark before he underwent anesthesia was he wanted to make sure that all of them were Republicans.

Q: Were they?

A: They said that today everyone is a Republican.

In that case, his wonderful sense of humor calmed a nation.

And then there was the time when the president was speaking to a group in the Rose Garden. It happened to coincide with a visit to my office by a couple of old college friends of mine, Paul and Molly Mahoney from California. I walked them out to the Rose Garden and we stood in the back near the press corps so they could actually see the president and Nancy. (Cautionary note: this will only be funny to people of a certain age.)

I noticed Molly looking at ABC's bad boy Sam Donaldson, who loved to be looked at. Sam had one of those sun-reflecting devices and he was turned with his back to the president and face to the sun, obviously soaking up rays while the president delivered a talk that was not in any form news-producing. Sam clearly was not taking notes. As we walked back along the colonnade toward my office afterward, I overheard Molly say to her husband: "That Garrick Utley sure didn't take the president's speech very seriously." I had tears in my eyes from laughing so hard.

Sam was a showman. To be mistaken for someone else, someone so different from Sam, would have at least momentarily crushed his ego.

Over the years, Sam and I found ourselves sharing a speaking platform now and again. The last time was at the memorial for my friend and business partner, Jody Powell. You can bet I often used that story of Sam's mistaken identity and you can bet he hated it! He occasionally came to the stage and pretended to choke me.

In truth, Sam was great fun off camera and we enjoyed teasing each other. One election day I walked into my polling place and his familiar voice rang out from across the crowded room, purportedly addressing the polling officials but commanding the attention of a long line of voters: "Gentlemen, check that lady's credentials. She is not old enough to vote."

It was simply impossible to get mad at Sam. Nancy had the same reaction. She just could not help laughing at him and teasing with him. That's when Sam, the serious newsman, would move in for the kill with a question meant to make you squirm.

There is such a pressure cooker environment when you work in the White House that humor is required to keep your equilibrium. Much of it is intemperate at best. We made fun of one another and ourselves. We pulled corny jokes on colleagues. No one was immune.

* * *

Mark Weinberg, an assistant press secretary in the West Wing, came to us fresh out of GW University. Mark always had a quirky sense of humor, which, I admit, we all encouraged.

He used to practice "forging" the handwriting of famous people and he'd often send one of us a fake letter from Nancy or Ronnie or some person of royalty. To encourage his habit, I brought him back some official stationery from one undisclosed royal chamber after an overseas trip. Mike Deaver found out about those letters and ordered an end to them, even though he issued that order with a definite note of amusement in his voice.

Mark could easily have been a stand-up comedian. He could imitate anyone. He had Nancy Reagan down to a tee. And you would swear it was Ronald Reagan on the phone when he called you. He could make everyone on the East Wing cry from laughing at his Ronnie and Nancy imitations.

Mark Weinberg wasn't the only comedian in the West Wing press office. The White House press office met early every morning. I never missed that meeting if I could help it, mostly because they were fun. Robin Gray, another assistant press secretary, could reduce us to tears with his antics. Joe Canzeri, an aide to Mike Deaver with a big ego, was often Robin's target. Joe was short; Robin was tall. On occasion Robin would come into the press office meeting walking on his knees and issuing "Canzeri-like" orders. Everyone encouraged his Joe Canzeri routine. All in good fun, making for great memories.

* * *

Nancy Reagan was a distant second to her husband in the humor business. He saw humor in just about everything. Her humor was a more gentle, refined, and understated variety.

At one event she was asked to be the one to introduce

President Reagan to the audience. She claimed it was the first time she'd done so. Then she asked the audience if they didn't think he looked pretty confident that she'd be able to handle it. The audience laughed appreciatively.

Then she began the introduction like this:

I'll tell you a little secret. He didn't look so confident when I was introducing him to my father for the first time.

Pretty good line. The audience loved it.

There was also an embarrassing incident one time when Nancy took to the microphone to introduce her husband. She got involved in some long story and moved back to sit down at the end of it while the audience politely applauded. Then she jumped up and explained she had forgotten to introduce the president. She called him her "roommate." The audience loved that one, too.

And then there was the unforgettable moment in Xi'an, China, where the famous Terracotta Warriors were being excavated after being discovered in 1974. The eight thousand or so life-sized warriors were created to honor Qin Shi Huang, the first Chinese emperor, and to protect him in the afterlife.

The president and First Lady were escorted down among the Terracotta Warriors to see these incredible objects up close and pose for a picture. President Reagan could not resist standing behind one of the headless warriors to make it look like he was the warrior. The press was behind a rope line about forty feet away. One short, heavyset, white-haired elderly "reporter" named Naomi Nover kept trying to get closer by ducking under the rope. I put the word *reporter* in quotes because Naomi didn't report for anyone that we knew of. Her deceased husband had been a one-person news bureau and he made Naomi his news reporter. Both got White House credentials. When he died, Naomi started attending the daily White House news briefings on her own. She paid for her single seat to take all the overseas trips, and once on board she tried to usurp two seats so that she could keep all her shopping bags full of her belongings next to her. It was an odd situation that went on until she died, some years after I had left the White House. I did everything I could to discourage her inclusion in our travels because it complicated everything, but she outlasted me.

Back to the story. The Chinese guards were having none of her moves. Finally, reporter Gary Schuster, White House reporter for the *Detroit News*, pulled out his wallet, took out a dollar bill, and showed the picture of George Washington to the guard, pointing from George to Naomi, obviously trying to tell him that Naomi was an important official who was on our paper money. Honestly, she was a dead ringer for George. The guard relented and let Naomi move up close. The press corps behind the ropes erupted in laughter.

20

Searching for Privacy

Everyone needs a little privacy now and then. But for First Families, privacy is a rare thing.

Nancy didn't complain about a lack of privacy in the White House. Perhaps because of her early career in Hollywood and her years as the wife of the governor of California she recognized it as a fact of life.

But some subjects—like her age—were touchy. Nancy's birthday was July 6. What year was the question.

I thought I was used to the pervasive climate of age denial among women during those years. My grandmother lived to be ninety-nine and lied about her age to the end. My own mother lied about her age. When she was seventy she filled out a form at her doctor's office listing her age as fifty. He must have been highly amused.

At the White House age took on a great deal more importance. Every year reporters would torture me with questions about Nancy's year of birth.

As all press secretaries know, the key to preserving your credibility when you are skeptical of information provided to you was to couch your response with something like this:

Mrs. Reagan tells me she was born in 1922, or
Mrs. Reagan tells me she is fifty-nine years old.

Nancy would occasionally add a casual mention to me that the unnamed hospital where she was born had burned down a long time ago along with all the hospital records. That felt like a step too far so I did not mention that to reporters. If I had, it might have become the first "birther" issue! Nancy Reagan, in fact, was born one year earlier than the date I was given.

At the beginning of the second Reagan administration, just weeks before I was planning to leave government service, I arranged for Nancy to be interviewed by Chris Wallace, then with NBC. He had a good relationship with her since she had known his dad, Mike, most of her life. Chris looked her in the eye and asked his first question.

"Mrs. Reagan, how old are you?" She paused before responding, "I haven't decided yet."

Afterward, I said to her, "You could have made my life so much easier if only you'd said that four years ago." Then we both started laughing.

The other person who made herself unavailable to the media in early July every year was Barbara Bush. Mrs. Bush went to Smith, as did Nancy. Barbara was born in 1925. If Nancy was born in 1922 as she claimed, they might have overlapped at Smith. But if Nancy was born in 1921, they would have missed each other. As far as I know, Mrs. Bush never responded to questions about whether or not they knew each other at Smith.

* * *

The ranch, Rancho del Cielo, was so important to the Reagans; it was their safe haven, a place where they could be relatively alone. A few days of relative privacy, horseback riding, and magnificent views were what they needed at the end of most nonstop months at the White House.

The conventional wisdom among members of the press corps was that Nancy was not fond of the ranch. But I know better. She dressed like a ranch hand; she rode daily with the president; she read a lot and, yes, she got on the phone, doing her best to keep close to her friends. She and the president also loved to sit outside where they could enjoy the fresh air and the solitude. John Barletta, the former Secret Service officer who served with them for seventeen years, says that it definitely was not true that Nancy disliked the ranch.

Former agent Barletta tells the story that one day while riding with him and President Reagan, Nancy inadvertently moved into heavy brush, so heavy it began to physically pull her off her horse. John had to leap off his horse and throw himself under her as she involuntarily slid off the horse and toward the ground. She got up, brushed herself off, and resumed riding. No drama.

When Nancy first started dating Ronnie, he was an avid tennis player. So she promptly went out and took tennis lessons. And when he rode, at least once a day, almost without exception, she rode. Nancy was just being Nancy, devoted, attentive, and putting Ronnie first.

The Queen of England came to visit the Reagans at the ranch. Because of heavy rains, the Queen's party had to travel by four-wheel drive instead of helicopter. It sounded like a harrowing drive from press reports, but I suspect the Queen was thoroughly charmed by the experience, at least in retrospect.

The relative privacy of the ranch was like a balm for the Reagans. I have a handwritten note from Nancy from July 13, 1994, in which she mentioned, "We're at the ranch at the moment where it's lovely—Had a beautiful ride this morning—Does all this sound familiar?"

* * *

The president's closest friends until the end were the two men who'd worked for him for years. Dennis LeBlanc and Barney Barnett. Barney died before I had the chance to talk with him. Barney was devoted to Ronald Reagan, and Ronald Reagan considered Barney indispensable. He lived at the ranch and cared for every detail of its management.

Dennis LeBlanc worked as part of the Reagan team for twenty-six years. No one knew Ronald and Nancy Reagan better than he did. Their relationship began in 1971 when he was assigned by the Highway Patrol as security for Governor Ronald Reagan. He then served in many tours and advance capacities for Reagan, on and off, until he won the presidency.

In 1980, the ranch became the new president's official residence and the president turned to Dennis for help. Dennis acted as his liaison with the government agencies responsible for bringing massive communications and physical security apparatus to the ranch. President Reagan's only guidance to Dennis was that nothing was to disturb the tranquility of the ranch.

Dennis was always at the ranch when the Reagans visited. "When we weren't building or repairing fences, we were clearing riding trails," explained Dennis. He said that in all that time, the president never cut down a living tree. Only if they were diseased or fallen did they make it into the woodpile. The only limbs cut were those that blocked passage along the trails. Every piece of wood they cut was used for firewood.

The Reagans, Dennis, and Barney had breakfast together at 7:15 a.m. daily. The fellows would move to the tack room about 9:00 a.m. where they would get the horses ready to ride. President Reagan always tacked up his own horse. When the horses were ready, President Reagan rang the bell outside the tack room to call Nancy to join them. They generally rode for two hours. Back by 11:00 a.m.

The president would ring the bell at the house at noon for Dennis and Barney to come to their forty-five-minute lunch. And then from one to four or four thirty in the afternoon, the president, Dennis, and Barney would clear the trails and chop wood.

Dennis said the ranch was where both the Reagans felt completely relaxed. The president read his daily briefings and handled his paperwork from the White House in mornings and evenings, but in between there was never any talk of business. The trail-clearing team told jokes and talked about day-to-day things.

And then, according to Dennis, they were called in for dinner, which was from 6:15 to 7:00 p.m. Promptly at 7:00 p.m. they watched *Murder She Wrote* and another show. Bedtime was exactly at 9:00 p.m. Sometimes, especially in the winter, the Reagans were in their nightclothes during dinner and TV viewing.

Dennis remembers that Nancy loved to talk through meals. President Reagan would secretly turn off his hearing aids during dinner and nudge Dennis with his foot as a signal that they were off; if Nancy directed a question to her husband, Dennis would use his own foot to nudge President Reagan. President Reagan would then say, "Darn it, Nancy, what did you say? These hearing aids aren't working right."

* * *

The president was diagnosed with Alzheimer's at the Mayo Clinic in August 1994, a month after her note to me. Family and friends had been noticing changes in 1993.

In November 1994, he wrote his powerful public letter telling America of his disease. Immediately, I heard speculation that he probably didn't write that letter himself. In fact, I jumped all over a female member of Congress when she said that in my presence. I hope I made her feel like a creep because that was my intent. She didn't even know him. Everyone who knew him knew better. No one but Ronald Reagan could have written that letter.

His last visit to the ranch was in August 1995.

The ranch was later sold to the Young Americas Foundation, which has preserved it. Dennis said the decision to sell was a difficult one for Nancy. But once the president could no longer ride, it made no sense to hold on to it. Dennis spent two weekends there with Nancy so that they could go through every book on the shelves to remove any inscriptions. He said Nancy, the protector in chief, did not want anyone buying the ranch to profit from those personally inscribed items. The ranch was being sold as-is, so the books themselves would have to stay.

Dennis had almost the exact same view of Nancy's feelings for the ranch as Agent John Barletta. "She went to the ranch because he loved it. She warmed to it for its peace and quiet." Privacy.

21

Staff Memories

Most Reagan White House staffers, like me, have many memories and stories from their years of service. I knew I needed to talk to as many of them as possible for this book. Our conversations became trips down memory lane and I am so glad for readers to be able to share in those trips.

It seemed only appropriate to begin a chapter of "Staff Memories" by hearing from our first chief of staff.

JIM BAKER, CHIEF OF STAFF, 1981–85

Jim Baker came to his job in a very roundabout way. During the last month of the 1980 presidential campaign, Reagan operatives Stu Spencer and Mike Deaver began to consider what a Reagan White House staff should look like and the name James A. Baker III kept coming up. The same James Baker had been Gerald Ford's delegate chairman during the last contested Republican convention in 1976 against Ronald

Reagan. The convention had been a real cliffhanger and Ford prevailed. So did bitter memories. Four years later Baker reappeared, again as a member of the opposition's team, chairing George H.W. Bush's campaign against Reagan for the presidency. It would be highly unusual to bring such an ardent opponent into the Reagan camp, let alone make him chief of staff.

Secretary Baker credits his appointment to a fortuitous last-minute trip to the men's room before a 1980 Republican primary debate. In the basement of the debate site, Jim Baker crossed paths with Nancy Reagan, who was on her way to the ladies' room. He stopped and introduced himself since they had never met before and he definitely made a good impression.

When Stu Spencer and Mike Deaver raised Jim Baker's name to the president-elect as a prospective chief of staff, Nancy was intrigued. Stu and Mike invited Jim on the president-elect's airplane a few times during the transition to give the Reagans a chance to feel him out. Jim became the linchpin of the first-term Reagan White House. We all admired and respected him for both his organizational wizardry and his good judgment.

Secretary Baker knew Nancy Reagan as someone who always operated as Ronald Reagan's protector. She was Ronald Reagan's eyes and ears. He says that she was pragmatic, with great instincts regarding personnel and public relations.

Secretary Baker described Ronald Reagan to me as a "wonderful, beautiful human being," his voice softening when he spoke those words. "Ronald Reagan was someone who would not swat a fly and really needed Nancy's insights. He could not bring himself to fire anyone."

The chief of staff vividly recalls the first time President Reagan debated Walter Mondale in 1984. President Reagan performed poorly and Nancy was, to say the least, upset. Stu Spencer, Mike Deaver, and Paul Laxalt all wanted Baker to fire Dick Darman, whom they blamed with stuffing President Reagan full of far too much detail. Secretary Baker told me "Dick Darman was not to blame and I refused to fire him." With a smile in his voice he remembered that he noticed a bit of "coolness" from Nancy for a while after that.

Secretary Baker has come to believe that the chief of staff job should have a two-year expiration date. He said he was "bone tired" when Don Regan proposed they swap jobs, with Baker becoming Treasury secretary after he'd been on the job more than four years. Both the Reagans and Mike Deaver took the suggestion without much argument. The swap took place.

The retirement years have not arrived for Secretary Baker who still practices law and a little politics at his Houston law firm. He said that he never went to California without stopping to see the Reagans and, after President Reagan's death, to visit with Nancy. When I asked him what he missed since she died, he said he really misses talking to her. So say we all.

KEN DUBERSTEIN, CHIEF OF STAFF, 1988

Ken Duberstein joined the Reagan White House Legislative Affairs shop in 1981 and helped lead Ronald Reagan's stellar legislative program. And as the campaign for reelection began to organize, Ken informed Chief of Staff Jim Baker that he was going to leave to work on the 1984 reelection campaign, coordinating congressional support on behalf of the president.

Jim told him that he needed to tell Nancy. Mike Deaver reinforced Jim's advice, telling Ken he needed to write Nancy a note explaining his reasons. Nancy hated losing staffers with whom she had become close. She never made it easy.

After about a week of silence, Ken described how he approached Nancy in a receiving line and she told him that while she accepted his decision she did not like the idea because he would be "too far away."

In February 1987, when Howard Baker assumed the chief of staff position, in the midst of the Iran-Contra controversy, Ken returned as his deputy, ultimately moving up to become chief of staff during the last year of the Reagan presidency. When I asked him how he was recruited to return to the White House, Ken says that to this day he still doesn't know who planted the idea of bringing him back because both Bob Strauss and Stu Spencer claim credit for planting the idea with Nancy Reagan whose "eyes lit up" at the prospect.

Ken was in the middle of a speech at the Capitol Hill Club when someone handed him a note to please call Kathy Osbourne, the president's secretary, immediately. He was asked to come to the Oval Office that afternoon to see the president.

When he got there, the president was alone in the Oval Office. The president looked at Ken and said, "I know all the reasons you gave Howard for why you can't come back but I want you to know that Nancy and I both want you back here for our last two years." And later, after the news broke that Ken was returning to the White House, Nancy called him and said, "Welcome home, Ken."

Nancy usually called Ken each weekday morning, often telling him what seemed to be on the president's mind.

Duberstein said Nancy's calls were always insightful and he welcomed them. He said her calls came when she had questions or sometimes with a suggestion to offer. Never to demand or dictate anything. Ken's observation was that both Ronald Reagan and Nancy Reagan were at their best when the other was involved.

When Nancy had breast cancer surgery and was recovering at the White House, she got the painful message that her mother had died. She told Ken they needed to leave for Phoenix the next Monday, just a few days later.

Ken explained that the president was speaking on Tuesday at West Point and that they would change the schedule to get them to Phoenix Tuesday evening after his speech and in time for the funeral. Changing the president's schedule is something akin to moving mountains, but Ken went to work and made all the adjustments.

As they lifted off on Marine One, with Nancy holding hands with the president, she turned to Ken with tears in her eyes and quietly said, "Thank you." She knew what a gargantuan effort it took to rearrange everything in such short order.

Once Ken was back in the White House, Nancy went to "work" on him. He became one of her "projects" as we used to say. She introduced him to friends, like Kay Graham. And thanks to her introduction, Ken became close with composer/entertainer Marvin Hamlisch. She called Marvin and Ken her "two Jewish sons."

Marvin invited both the Dubersteins and the Reagans to his wedding in New York one Memorial Day weekend. Nancy was not able to get to New York in time for the wedding but did arrive later that day. As usual, she stayed at the Carlyle

Hotel. So Ken and Marvin paraded Marvin's new bride, Terri, down Park Avenue to the hotel, carrying her train behind her.

Ken remembers when Don Regan's book hit the shelves and, in addition to the disclosure about astrology, Regan wrote that Nancy was still accepting designer clothes. Ken walked into the Oval Office to alert the president so that he could tell his wife. The president looked at Ken and said, "Why don't you tell her?" That sounded more than a little familiar to me.

Anyway, Ken did his duty. Later that evening, around 11:00 p.m., Nancy called him and said with a tinge of exasperation in her voice, "I am going through my entire closet and cataloging every single one of them."

During the last months of the administration, whenever the Reagans were in town and available on Friday evenings, Ken organized a "family film festival" complete with popcorn and showings of old films for an audience of friends and fellow staffers. *Hellcats of the Navy* and *Bedtime for Bonzo* were two of the films Ken remembers being shown in the family theater. Before each movie the president stood up and spent a few minutes telling the audience about how the film was shot and other anecdotes. When they showed *Hellcats of the Navy*, President Reagan got up at the beginning and explained that this was the only movie he and Nancy made together and the first time he actually kissed her. They then proceeded to reenact it for their delighted guests.

NANCY REYNOLDS, TRANSITION DIRECTOR FOR NANCY REAGAN

Nancy Reynolds's relationship with the Reagans goes back to the 1960s, when she was coanchoring the CBS News in San Francisco as a political reporter. It is no surprise the Reagans loved her; she actually interviewed Ronald Reagan on horseback. When Ronald Reagan won his campaign for governor, she accepted the job of assistant press secretary for radio and television and moved to Sacramento.

Within her first month on the job, Nancy Reynolds met Nancy Reagan. Reynolds had been sent to the airport by Lyn Nofziger, press secretary, to get on a plane with Nancy and travel with her to Los Angeles. They boarded the plane and were seated up front. Within minutes, two men seated behind them started criticizing Ronald Reagan's budget. The quiet First Lady of California, as Nancy Reynolds described her, came "alive." She stood up, looked these guys in the eye, and started in. "That's my husband you're talking about!" And then she went on to point out that, with regards to the budget, they "didn't know what they were talking about."

"That's when I knew Nancy Reagan was a woman to be reckoned with," said Nancy Reynolds.

When Ronald Reagan made his first run for the presidency in 1976, Nancy Reynolds joined the staff as an "advance man" for the campaign, primarily in charge of advance work for Nancy Reagan. She remembers all the small towns and hard-to-reach places she visited with the candidate's wife. One of her favorites: Banner Elk, North Carolina, where the Republican ladies outdid themselves. They seemed to have found every Republican woman in the mountains of North Carolina and invited them to tea with Nancy. During their never-ending travels, these two women became friends. From that time forward, Nancy Reagan considered Nancy Reynolds indispensable.

Governor Ronald Reagan and Nancy wanted to welcome home the prisoners of war returning from Vietnam following the US pullout. Nancy enlisted help from Nancy Reynolds to help her organize five different events—celebratory dinners, three in Los Angeles and two in Sacramento.

The Justin Darts, close personal friends of the Reagans, opened their spacious home for the three welcome-home events in Los Angeles. Nancy Reynolds remembers when Everett Alvarez gave Nancy Reagan his tin cup that he brought home from his years of imprisonment. It was the only thing he was allowed to keep in his cell.

Many of the returnees required hospitalization. Nancy visited every area hospital treating Vietnam casualties, spending a lot of time with each patient. She never failed to ask about their families and how to reach them. She always followed up, talked to the families, and gave them details about her visit and the young man's health.

During that bloody war, many Americans at home wore "bracelets" with the name of one of the Americans imprisoned by the North Vietnamese.

It was at one of those welcome-home dinners that Governor Reagan first met John McCain whose bracelet he'd worn during all of John's years in captivity.

Nancy Reynolds was the daughter of Democratic congress-man and senator D. Worth Clark from Idaho. She was familiar with the ways of Washington. She knew everyone and every-one knew—and liked—her. She literally lived in Blair House for months during the transition while helping the incoming First Lady find and hire staff. Between Nancy and Tish Bal-dridge, who had been Jackie Kennedy's social secretary, Nancy had the help to assemble a first-rate team. They even recom-mended me!

During the transition, it is customary for the outgoing First Lady to take the incoming First Lady on a tour of the private quarters so she could begin to plan their move. Mike Deaver insisted that Nancy Reynolds accompany him, Lyn Nofziger, and Nancy Reagan on the tour followed by a tea. Nancy Reynolds said Rosalynn seemed "frosty" as she showed them all the rooms—except one. Nancy Reagan asked about the room they hadn't seen and Rosalynn was obviously re-luctant to show it to them. The incoming First Lady asked which room it was and Rosalynn said it was the master bed-room. Nancy insisted she really needed to see it and Rosalynn opened it with great reluctance. Apparently, there were mov-ing boxes stacked up around that room and she didn't want to show it to anyone.

Later, Paul Costello, Rosalynn's White House press secre-tary, would mention to me that the election loss was very hard on Rosalynn and this tour was personally painful for her.

Nancy Reynolds has a million stories but none more inter-esting than having been at the White House with the First Lady when Donald Regan hung up on her. As Nancy Reynolds left the White House that day she ran into Chris Wallace out on Pennsylvania Avenue. She told him what had just happened. Chris made a beeline back to the TV studio and the country heard about the infamous hang-up within hours.

Here is my perspective on these events:

Donald Regan and Jim Baker swapped jobs in the second Reagan term. Don became chief of staff and Jim became Treasury secretary. At the same time, Nancy's trusted friend Mike Deaver left government to start his own firm. Nancy assumed she could take her questions and concerns to the new chief of staff. Wrong assumption.

Don Regan, in advance of the November 1985 summit meeting between President Reagan and General Secretary Gorbachev, gave a strange interview to Donnie Radcliffe, *Washington Post* Style reporter, who asked him questions about the upcoming meeting of these two world leaders. Regan told her he doubted most women would understand the importance of topics such as "throw weights or what's happening in Afghanistan or what is happening in human rights."

Instead, the new chief of staff went on to say that most women would rather read about "the human-interest stuff of what happened," alluding to social teas or lunches featuring Mrs. Reagan and Mrs. Gorbachev. Yikes!

Those patronizing comments from Donald Regan explain to me his reaction to Nancy's calls to him. After Mike Deaver left the White House, she no longer had someone on staff to talk to about things that were worrying her. Instead of recognizing her legitimate concerns, Donald Regan tried to have her redirect her calls to one of his deputies. He couldn't be bothered. He was sure the First Lady wouldn't understand the complexities of the issue she may have called him about.

I vividly remember a lunch at the vice president's residence when I was seated next to Mr. Regan about six months into his new position. He told me that Nancy's calls annoyed him and he was thinking of hiring one of "her socialite friends" who could sit at a desk outside his office and take her calls. I bit my lip and did not respond, but that is when I knew he was going to run into troubled waters.

Donald Regan's abrupt and graceless departure came within forty-eight hours of the news breaking on NBC that he had hung up the phone on the First Lady. I am fairly certain that, never in White House history, had a First Lady been treated so cavalierly. Mr. Regan really left himself defenseless once the media "feeding frenzy" began. How can you justify such rude behavior? By all accounts, once Ronald Reagan learned about it by watching Chris Wallace announce it on the evening newscast, he was appalled. He asked Nancy if it was true and she told him it was. As press speculation mounted about how long Mr. Regan could remain in the chief of staff position, the White House communications apparatus stayed ominously quiet. The chief of staff submitted his resignation to the president, it was accepted, and Donald Regan left immediately.

MUFFIE BRANDON

The year was 1981 and it was early in the Reagan administration. Muffie Brandon was notified at the last minute that

Prince Charles was soon to enter the White House through the Diplomatic Reception Room facing the South Lawn. He was in Washington for a private visit and made plans to stop by to pay a quick visit with the Reagans. As Muffie recalls it was a Saturday. In her own words:

I was in rather casual clothes as I had planned to spend the day at my desk preparing for the next week's events.

There were no fresh flowers in the Diplomatic Reception Room (called "The Dip Room" by staff) and the florist was out.

I raced over to the vice president's office and asked his assistant if the vice president had any fresh flowers in his office. We knocked and there he was with a fine bouquet on a side table. I quickly explained the situation, lusting in my heart for those flowers, and asked if I could "borrow" them for a few hours until the prince left. VP Bush said, "Sure, take 'em but don't forget to bring them back" with a twinkle in his eye. I was racing against time, and time was winning. We were on the final countdown.

Back to the Dip Room at full speed; pop the vase on the large table just as the limousine draws up to the door. The head usher was standing by to escort the prince to the private quarters upstairs.

Just as I was figuring how to make myself invisible, Julius comes walking into the reception room. Julius was Mrs. Reagan's hairdresser. He'd obviously just come from the residence and was on his way out the same door the prince was about to enter. A definite no-no.

I grabbed Julius and pushed him into a broom closet across the hall among the brooms, vacuum cleaners, and mops. I jumped in right behind him and quietly closed the door. I stayed alert to the possibility that, at a moment's notice, I might have to slap my hand across the mouth of the ebullient hairdresser.

While it seemed like forever, some minutes later, Chief Usher Rex Scouten knocked discreetly on the door and whispered that "the coast is clear."

Flowers were promptly returned to the vice president's office.

Mission complete.

Nancy would have been pleased by the attentiveness paid to make the prince's visit go smoothly. If only she knew how close the prince came to meeting a social secretary dressed in jeans and the First Lady's hairdresser who was perfectly capable of asking him for his autograph if the spirit moved him. These are the kinds of near misses Nancy seldom if ever learned about . . . at least if we could help it.

FRED RYAN, WHITE HOUSE—PRESIDENTIAL SCHEDULING, CHIEF OF STAFF, OFFICE OF THE FORMER PRESIDENT

Fred vividly remembers when President Reagan was thrown from a horse at a friend's ranch in Mexico. One of the first things Nancy did when they needed to helicopter the former president to the hospital was to ask Fred to reach all four of the Reagan kids so they would not learn of this first from the news. Clearly, she was remembering how Melissa Brady heard an erroneous radio report announcing her dad's death when Jim was shot on March 30. Melissa was a college student in Colorado and she flew to DC believing that her father was dead.

He said Nancy was the head cheerleader for the Reagan Library in later years. She raised huge amounts of money for the library endowment; she came to every meeting, to every event, and prodded staff to keep raising money. She kept a list of everyone she wanted contacted and she followed up on those prospects. Both Reagans tried to keep current connections in Hollywood with folks like Tom Cruise, Katie Holmes, Warren Beatty, Sally Field, and Arnold Schwarzenegger, for instance, inviting them to events at the library, having lunch. The TV program *Veep* was filmed at the Reagan Library.

All this exposure creates buzz and enhances the reputation of the library.

Fred remembers that "Nancy was overwhelmed by the public outpouring of support after President Reagan released his letter telling the country about his Alzheimer's. Bags and bags of mail poured in; at least a hundred letters were from people who wanted to offer ideas about possible cures."

The reaction inspired her to make the disease her main cause. She spoke often about Alzheimer's on television and in appearances with people like Michael J. Fox and Larry King. She worked with several different Alzheimer's groups, lending her name to help with fund-raising, especially her own Nancy Reagan Research Institute. In helping her husband, she helped so many others.

MARLIN FITZWATER, PRESS SECRETARY

Marlin Fitzwater is one of the top press secretaries who ever graced the White House. His job never went to his head, saving him from the "Potomac Fever" many acquire. And he knew how to walk the tightrope involved in working for the president and serving the needs of the press.

Marlin had been the deputy press secretary between 1983 and 1984. He moved up into the position of the press secretary to Vice President Bush until 1987 when Don Regan talked him into returning as White House press secretary.

Marlin was only a few months into his new position when the *Washington Post* ran a story insinuating that the First Family wanted Donald Regan to step down from the post of chief of staff. Nancy called Marlin and told him not to involve himself in the story at all, just to "leave it alone." Within weeks, Donald Regan resigned abruptly with a one-sentence resignation letter that he handed to Marlin and told him to issue. Marlin was stunned but did as instructed without anyone giving him any guidance on what the backstory was. This all happened after Regan hung up the phone on Nancy.

Marlin told me a story he'd never told before. It was 1987 and the Gorbachevs were arriving for a visit, coming up the circular driveway on the South Grounds. Normally the president and Mrs. Reagan would greet their guests outside as their car pulled up. Because of extreme cold, they were waiting for them inside the Diplomatic Reception Room along with a crowd of people who were part of the welcoming ceremony. When the Gorbachevs walked in, Nancy noticed immediately that Raisa's panty hose were collapsing around her ankles. She walked over to Raisa quickly, stood close as they shook hands, and whispered, "Come with me," escorting her around the corner into the ladies' room. They emerged a few minutes later and no one ever noticed their disappearance. Marlin said, "I thought at the time that Nancy had done more for US-Russian relations with that one gesture than had been accomplished since the creation of the Soviet Union."

Marlin also told me about the day Nancy called him to tell him she was scheduled to undergo breast cancer surgery and she wanted him to make the announcement in a matter-of-fact manner. Marlin said those were the days when no one even said the word *breast* on television, let alone discussed the details of one's surgery. He did his homework on the disease and handled the announcement. Afterward, Nancy thanked him for the dignified way he had handled it. She asked him if there were any lingering questions. He explained that some of the press were asking why she had a mastectomy instead of a lumpectomy. The doctor's daughter looked Marlin in the eye and said, "You tell them this: I want to live." No reporter ever followed up with him on this question so he never delivered this answer. He said to me that her death of heart failure at age ninety-four "proved she made the right decision for her own health."

When the president had a basal cell carcinoma on his face removed, the procedure called a rhomboid flap was used. President Reagan was, according to Marlin, very self-conscious about how it looked. Marlin told him that he'd had one when he was young with a graft from behind his ear and that you couldn't even tell he'd had surgery a month later.

But, he told the president, "It improved my sex life by 45 percent."

Later when the president's operation had healed, he was talking with someone in the Oval Office and he expressed his satisfaction with the surgery. He then looked over at Marlin and said, "And I hope I have the same results as Marlin." They both laughed.

LANDON PARVIN

Former White House speechwriter Landon Parvin took a call from the president's personal secretary, Kathy Osborne, telling him that the president would like to begin the process of preparing a speech to the nation as soon as the Tower Commission released its report on the Iran-Contra affair. That report would be released on February 26, 1987. The president wanted Landon to be the writer.

The mood in the White House and in Washington had been one of crisis as the arms-for-hostages deal, which included a diversion of Iranian funds to support the Nicaraguan Contras, had become known. The president's poll numbers had dropped, and scandal was in the air with White House officials under investigation. Admiral John Poindexter, the president's national security adviser, and an NSC aide, Colonel Oliver North, had either resigned or been fired. Questions were raised about the role of the president's chief of staff, Don Regan. What did the secretary of state and the secretary of defense know of the plan?

With visions of Watergate in his head, Landon immediately

called Nancy to ask her a very simple question. He said, "Who can I trust?"

Who could he trust to help him navigate the various currents that were swirling? Who had no ax to grind, no interests to protect, and wasn't looking to save himself at the expense of the president? She didn't hesitate. She said, "David Abshire."

Dr. Abshire, the former ambassador to NATO, had been named special counselor to the president with cabinet rank. He had been tapped to lead the Reagan administration response to the crisis. He insisted on complete transparency.

Landon told Nancy he would immediately go see Dr. Abshire and would begin talking to others but that he would also need to talk to the president at some point after the report was released. Nancy said, "Tell me when."

The report was released on a Thursday and Landon left a message for Nancy that he needed to see the president. On Friday, Landon's phone rang and the White House operator said, "I have Mrs. Reagan on the line." He gave her a rundown on what he had been hearing from people on what the president needed to say. He was especially concerned that the White House legal counsel wanted the president to take a narrow, specific approach to what had happened. Just a few weeks before, Nancy had gotten into an argument with Don Regan on the very same thing. Regan had wanted the president to do a news conference after the report was released where he would have been peppered with specific questions, the substance of which the president was not well versed on. She knew a legalistic approach was not the answer. She told Landon, "There will be a meeting this evening at five thirty in the residence— you, two other men, and Ronnie. No one knows about it."

Driving to the White House that evening, Landon heard on the radio that the former senator from Tennessee, Howard Baker, was to be the new chief of staff and that an enraged Don Regan had fired off a one-sentence letter of resignation.

Landon, alone, was cleared into the White House through the East Gate. He went directly to the private residence.

It was not Howard Baker at the meeting, however, but the report's chairman, John Tower, and Stu Spencer, the president's longtime political adviser. Landon wondered who had arranged this. When President Reagan thanked former senator Tower for taking on this difficult assignment, which proved to be critical of the president, Tower choked up.

Landon said, "Contrary to some reports about this meeting, Senator Tower showed no signs of having been drinking. I thought this was one of the nicer moments I had seen in Washington—when the man who had just issued a report critical of the president was thanked by the president himself for his work. I understood Senator Tower's emotional reaction."

Nancy was present for some of the discussion, but she slipped in and out to watch how the evening news was covering the Regan/Baker story. She listened intently when she was there. Standing up to leave, the group lamented the recent suicide attempt of the president's previous national security adviser, Bud McFarlane, who felt he had let the country down. Everyone, including the president, agreed he was a decent and conscientious man.

Landon recalls what a painful time it was in the Reagan administration. He credits the thoughtful guidance of Dr. Abshire and President Reagan's desire to take full responsibility as the reason the ship of state was righted. I think Landon's expert speechcraft provided ballast as well.

Landon credits the quiet influence of Nancy Reagan with having been an important element in the final resolution. He believes she was an expert judge of people, including her own husband, at a time when that is exactly what the White House and the Reagan presidency needed.

MARK WEINBERG

Mark was a two-termer, with the Reagans from start to finish and then in California after they left Washington, DC. Here are several of his favorite moments with Nancy:

"Mrs. Reagan loved her husband for who he was, but his good looks were not lost on her. He was, after all, handsome. She especially liked his full head of hair. I remember two different stories about that. Once, during the White House years, she and Larry Speakes were looking at the president's schedule, and trying to find time for an event she wanted him to do. Larry suggested that the president's haircut could be moved to make room but Mrs. Reagan quickly shot him down. 'Larry,' she said firmly, 'Ronnie cannot look scruffy.'

"In 1989, former president Reagan was operated on for a subdural hematoma caused when he was thrown by a wild horse he was riding a few months earlier. Doctors shaved his head to access the injury site. Shortly after the surgery began, I remember seeing Mrs. Reagan in a waiting room holding a plastic bag filled with hair, and I asked her what it was. She said, 'It's Ronnie's. I told them to give it to me. I want to be able to prove that he does not dye it.' Or, I wondered, if maybe she was worrying about someone selling it! Stranger things have happened. A few days later, when he was about to be discharged from the hospital, President Reagan was given a baseball cap to conceal his very short haircut. At first he did not want to wear it—he saw nothing wrong with how he looked—but Mrs. Reagan insisted. She did not like how it looked. He gave in. Until, that is, he boarded the small private plane that would take us back to Los Angeles. Just before he entered the cabin, President Reagan took off his hat and gave a big wave to the assembled press. Mrs. Reagan was horrified and tried to cover up his head with her hand, but to no avail."

BARBARA COOK FABIANI, DEPUTY PRESS SECRETARY TO THE FIRST LADY

Barbara worked on the George H.W. Bush 1980 campaign against Ronald Reagan. When she applied for a job in the first Reagan administration, she had a lot of competition from women who had worked for Ronald Reagan's press secretary, Lyn Nofziger. In the end I decided to hire Barbara because I could tell she knew what she was doing and would help me the most. I never regretted that decision. Another lifelong friend.

In April 1983, President Reagan's Interior secretary, James Watt, announced that "rock bands attract the wrong element" and banned the Beach Boys from playing on the National Mall on the Fourth of July. The press went wild.

When Nancy Reagan heard the news, she told her press office to call the press and tell them that "Nancy Reagan loves the Beach Boys." She had real affection for the California-based band.

At this time Barbara was engaged to a man named Jim, so when a receptionist announced that Jim was on the phone, Barbara answered, "Hello, honey!" Wrong Jim.

It was Jim Watt—a very nervous Jim Watt—who wanted to know if Nancy did in fact have a special relationship with the Beach Boys. Barbara gave him a definitive yes and the short-lived Beach Boys ban was quickly rescinded.

Barbara remembers that after the Beach Boys played the July 4th event, Nancy invited them to a return engagement on the South Lawn in honor of the Special Olympics.

Barbara recalls that "the next time I answered a call involving the Beach Boys was in December 1983, when Dennis Wilson accidentally drowned off the California coast and his family wanted to honor his wish to be buried at sea. They had learned that only Coast Guard and Navy veterans had that right and were asking Nancy to intercede. Dennis Wilson was buried at sea."

Barbara, as Nancy's press advance person, had to be quick on her feet and able to professionally represent the First Lady's interests as she worked her way through competing interests and large egos.

Here is her account of one particularly sensitive assignment:

During the 1980s, one of the largest Republican contributors was Ross Perot, the founder of EDS (Electronic Data Systems) in Dallas, Texas. He was a forceful presence.

By February 1982, Mrs. Reagan was traveling extensively to focus on the devastating effects of drugs on young people. She was meeting with a wide selection of people and hearing firsthand experiences. Dallas was one of the stops. Several weeks prior, I traveled to Texas to visit various groups, including several recommended by Ross Perot. I thought a knowledgeable group called Richardson (Texas) Families in Action was perfect. They would give Mrs. Reagan useful insight into the war on drugs from a grassroots level. Little did I realize this was not the organization Mr. Perot had in mind. It seems he had already made promises to others. He had also made promises for interviews with local media without consulting the press office, let alone Nancy Reagan.

He invited me over to EDS headquarters to explain my choice and told me I was dead wrong. Finally, in his Texas drawl he said, "Little lady, you go over there in a private office and call the White House. You let them know they will meet with my group."

Stunned, I slowly dialed my office wondering how to deal with this powerful fellow. As I was speaking to Sheila Tate, she told me that Ross Perot was on another phone speaking directly to Nancy Reagan about the matter. I thought this was the end but Nancy Reagan stood by me telling Perot she trusted the judgment of her staff. This took real courage.

Barbara also tells a funny story about protecting Nancy and the president from poisoned food:

Every president travels with a personal aide who oversees all food preparation before the president is allowed to eat it. President Reagan was no exception. We were staying at the Century Plaza Hotel in Los Angeles and I decided to make a quick run through the presidential suite before their arrival. Much to my surprise, the doors were wide open and a Century Plaza bellman was inside holding an overflowing food basket from a place called Mrs. Beasley's Bakery. The bellman explained a stranger hurried up to him in the lobby and paid him to take the basket to the president's suite. The card read: "Loved seeing you on TV this morning. Ray and Fran." Names I did not recognize.

Some of this made sense since Mrs. Reagan had been on *Good Morning America* that morning, but visions of a crazy person sending something dangerous to eat passed through my mind. So I took the basket away and placed it in the staff office, never giving it another thought. The food turned out to be fine since no staffers got sick.

Several weeks later, back at the White House, Elaine Crispin, Nancy's personal secretary, came into my office asking if I'd seen any gifts from the famous LA producer Ray Stark (*West Side Story, Funny Girl, Steel Magnolias, Annie*) and his wife, Fran. Sheepishly, I explained my bungled attempt at protection. Mrs. Reagan laughed when she heard what happened and quickly sent a thank-you note to the senders for the food that her staff had devoured.

MARY ANNE FACKELMAN, OFFICIAL PHOTOGRAPHER

Mary Anne, a career government employee/photographer, was assigned to First Lady Rosalynn Carter and pivoted to cover Nancy after the 1980 election. She was a real pro.

Maf had an uncanny ability to snap a picture without anyone being aware of her presence; she also had an incredible eye. She caught every emotion. Nancy didn't need to see many of her photos before she knew she wanted Maf, as we came to call her, as part of our team.

One of Mary Anne's many memories was how Nancy handled photo approval. We all used to laugh about it. If for any reason Nancy did not like a picture, she tore off the top right corner.

Here are some of Mary Anne's observations:

She always photographed so beautifully and was at ease in front of the cameras. This made life so much easier and enabled me to focus on trying to get the shots that I knew we would need for "thank you's" or for general release.

I watched her deal with people who were excited to meet her and simultaneously intimidated by the experience. She put them at ease with a touch or a smile or a question.

I was with her in a number of intimate, emotional moments. When we flew west, she always stopped to visit her mother in Arizona. In the early days, I noticed that Mrs. Reagan appeared almost in awe of her mother and solicitous to her. She brought her flowers and laughed at her many jokes. As her mother failed, Mrs. Reagan was quiet and observant during her visits. When her mother died, I will never forget the cry of anguish I heard when Mrs. Reagan saw her at the mortuary for the first time. Her pain was palpable and deep.

When Patti was getting married, Mrs. Reagan helped her plan a grand wedding. I was cautious about photography before and during the wedding because I was aware of Patti's preference for privacy. One example: I recall being in the cottage at the hotel and came upon Mrs. Reagan sitting on the side of the bed talking quietly with Patti before either of them got dressed. It was so clear that she was taking that special moment to talk to her daughter privately. I took a photo as quietly as I could but it has never been released out of respect for their privacy.

My time during the Reagan years was filled with more official state visits than I can count and days that were packed with arrival ceremonies on the South Lawn. Most of the time I would be working with a reciprocal photographer from the visiting head of state; I had to remember to gesture when language was a barrier as well as working around and behind interpreters.

One moment sticks out in my memory. I was teaching a new photographer named Susan what the drill was for taking pictures during the "handshake line." The new photographer was moving in too closely, which I knew Mrs. R would not appreciate, so I attempted to stage-whisper "Susan, take a step back." No problem except that our guest that evening was Hosni Mubarak of Egypt and his wife, Susan. She heard my instructions and promptly took several steps back.

And to make matters worse, our new photographer was removing film from her camera to reload when the film flipped out of her hands and flew under Mrs. Reagan's gown. I tiptoed up to Nancy and said, "Excuse me while I remove a roll of film that is on the floor under your gown." I got "the look."

The excitement surrounding the dinner for Prince Charles and Princess Diana was not to be believed. Pete Souza and I were the two photographers who covered this historic visit. After the dinner, of course, dancing began. Pete got the best photo of Diana and John Travolta as they danced. What a night!

At the last minute, Mrs. Gorbachev decided to accompany her husband to New York for UN meetings involving President Reagan. That meant I needed to be there to photograph the ladies. Mrs. Gorbachev kept asking me to take one picture after another, which was prolonging our visit.

I was in the midst of planning my wedding and was under the gun to get to Toledo in time to meet the Ohio obligation to spend three days in residence before obtaining a marriage license.

Mrs. Reagan knew it and came to my rescue. She took my arm and announced, "This girl is getting married and must leave now," whereupon all conversation and photo requests stopped and I was sent on my way in a New York City police car with a local Secret Service agent accompanying me to get me through the lines and onto my plane.

How could you not love a woman who would do that for you?

Thanks to Nancy, Mary Anne became Mary Anne Fackelman-Miner and lives happily in Hawaii with her husband, Ray.

She reflected on her years:

Working as the First Lady's photographer was a great honor. I was able to travel the world with her. I recorded her visit with the emperor of Japan; the wedding of Charles and Diana; the wedding of Andrew and Sarah; the king of Thailand; the pope; the funeral of Princess Grace; trips to Singapore, Stockholm, Bali. And on and on. Nancy Reagan always represented our country beautifully.

I also saw the great vulnerability in her that she worked hard to mask from the public. The last night she and the president stayed in the White House, she called the photo office and asked me and Pete Souza to come up to the residence to say goodbye.

Last-minute packing was going on. We talked and exchanged personal recollections of favorite times and we finally got up to leave her to finish her packing. Our final hug from her was one that brought me to tears and a huge lump in my throat. She was crying too.

FRED FIELDING, WHITE HOUSE LEGAL COUNSEL

We called upon the White House Counsel's office regularly. Not that we wanted to. But when problems arose, Fred Fielding was the lawyer you wanted in your camp. Here are his memories:

Nancy Reagan could be a demanding and formidable force, but she was not "the Dragon Lady" as she was sometimes portrayed. She was opinionated to be sure, but more realistically, she was an elegant and thoughtful person whose sole purpose was to be the First Lady to her beloved president—and I came to truly believe all she did and said was in allegiance to that purpose.

As counsel to the president, my office served not only the president but also the constituent groups within the White House staff. Not the least of these was the East Wing, which was the domain of the First Lady and her staff. And, during the Reagan years, there was a wonderful assemblage of bright energized staffers that Nancy had handpicked, and it was, indeed, a very demanding and active "client" of my office.

Nancy was very engaged with the tasks and activities of her staff, and her demand for perfection to the slightest details made our work for her staff demanding as well. However, after a few false starts, I deployed a very handsome, soft-spoken senior associate counsel to be the East Wing staff's primary day-to-day contact, and things went fairly smoothly thereafter with the East Wing. My primary responsibility was the direct dealings with the First Lady.

Aside from the day-to-day tasks of the East Wing, and First Lady responsibilities, it became obvious to me early on that she had a slight blind spot when it came to scrupulous adherence to gift rules as they applied to her by law and by custom. One of my first assignments in early 1981 in that regard was a meeting with Mrs. Reagan in the residence, arranged and accompanied by Jim Baker and Ed Meese. The purpose, I was told, was for me to brief the First Lady, as she didn't understand my directions to the White House staff on the acceptance of gifts. That meeting was a painful half hour as she vehemently insisted that personal gifts to her and Ronnie would not possibly be covered by such rules. After the meeting, as we descended in the elevator from the living quarters, Jim and Ed were convulsed in laughter at my initiation into the "world of Nancy Reagan." Later we also had the press flap over the "acceptance" of designer clothes ("gown-gate"), until it was announced that she had only borrowed them and they would be returned or turned over to the Smithsonian. At that time she also made her singing debut at the Gridiron Dinner belting out "Second Hand Clothes" like a pro. But the persistent pressing issue was over gifts from close friends—she would say "but that wasn't a gift to the First Lady—it was personal to me from our friend Frank, etc." So, much to her annoyance, we had an annual trip to the residence to search and locate the "private gifts."

But it also became obvious to me from the start that Nancy's primary focus was the protection of "Ronnie." It was behind every inquiry and every request. And there were many. Sometimes they came up in a meeting with her in the residence. More often, it came in a phone call, which usually started with her slowly saying "Fred . . ." Sometimes it was a double "Fred . . . Fred . . ." A triple "Fred" call was reserved for the toughest issues, not a complaint over a policy or proposed activity, but her concern about someone in the government who was acting improperly, or in her mind, was taking advantage of "Ronnie" or who should be fired because they were hurting "Ronnie." These calls became the source of some amusement in my office, especially in the first two years, since I was trying to stop smoking and often I would relapse during or after a call from the East Wing. But, in fairness to Nancy, she was usually right in her assessment of a situation and often had seen the problem before anyone else. She could be very harsh in her candid assessments of people, but her motive was never a petty or personal one—it was always to protect the president.

And it should not be forgotten that she could also be very kind and thoughtful. To illustrate, by early 1986, I had heavily depleted our personal savings and was ready to resign. I met with the president and told him of my plans and he was very gracious. The next day, however, I was summoned to the residence and met by an angry First Lady who said she couldn't understand how I could desert Ronnie, just like Bill Smith, Bill Clark . . . and she named a string of others she felt had deserted the president. I explained my situation, but she didn't let up on me, and I left the meeting feeling depressed that in her eyes I had failed to be loyal to the president.

The next morning she telephoned me in my office;

I braced for a rerun. But to my surprise, she was soft-spoken and she told me she was calling to apologize for yelling at me. She had talked to Ronnie the previous evening and he had told her I had been the only one of all the original assistants to the president that had still remained on the staff, and that he was grateful I had given him so much time. She said she was just frustrated the day before, and now understood. And, for years after, at events with the president or events after his death, she was always gracious to me and my wife, including us in the events, and in conversations.

As I stated at the beginning, she was not "the Dragon Lady" but instead was a grand and gracious lady, who wanted only to protect her president—which she did in every way she could.

CAROL MCCAIN, DIRECTOR, WHITE HOUSE VISITORS OFFICE

Carol McCain loved Nancy. Carol and her husband at the time, Senator John McCain, knew Nancy from her involvement in the POW issues. She hosted many dinners for them in Sacramento and in Los Angeles.

Like many people who fell under Nancy's spell, Carol ended up joining the Reagan political campaigns and working for them. During the 1980 campaign, she was one of only two women on the staff of about twenty people managed by John Sears.

Carol described herself as a "Jack of all trades" doing whatever Nancy needed done. She laughs remembering an appearance at a Little League baseball game in Florida. Nancy sat down on the bench. Carol looked down and noticed Nancy had on one blue shoe and one black shoe. Nancy realized her fashion faux pas at the same time. They smiled at each other and pretended not to notice.

Carol also functioned as Nancy's press secretary during the campaign. And once, during the New Hampshire primary, Nancy complained about one particular well-worn dress that she kept having to wear. Ronald Reagan overheard and suggested, "Give it to Carol. She'd look good in it." Nancy stopped complaining; Carol did not get the dress. But it's fun to imagine the press reaction when they'd inevitably notice Carol was wearing a dress they'd photographed numerous times on Nancy out on the campaign trail.

MONA CHAREN, SPEECHWRITER

The First Lady's office was in desperate need of a full-time speechwriter. We had borrowed talent from the president's team for years and felt we needed someone who did nothing but work with the East Wing. And along came Mona!

Early in 1984 I was interviewed for the job of speechwriter for Nancy Reagan by Michael Deaver. His office was gorgeous. His desk was pristine. Not a paper in sight. Just carefully arranged blotter and pen holders and paperweights. Beautiful photos of the Reagans behind him. He told me that in all his years of working for the Reagans, he'd never been criticized by Ron, only by Nancy.

He stressed how tough she could be, what a demanding boss and so forth, and asked whether I was ready for that.

I had worked at *National Review* from 1979 to 1981. I left to spend a year in Israel and then go to law school. I'd done a good deal of writing for *National Review* and Bill and Priscilla Buckley recommended me to the White House after I graduated from law school.

I was just out of law school and was overwhelmed to be sitting in the West Wing of the White House. If Mike Deaver had said, "Listen you can have this job but we ask that you submit to waterboarding first," I would have said, "Sign me up."

The next step was meeting Mrs. Reagan. Because of what Mike Deaver had said, I was expecting a Dragon Lady. Instead, this diminutive, very polite lady met me at the elevator and escorted me to the sunroom. I don't know how old she was then, maybe in her sixties? But I was struck by two things: she was girlish and gracious at the same time. I don't remember what we talked about. I do remember that she offered me chocolates and I thought to myself, *She doesn't look like she ever indulges in chocolates!*

Fast-forward to my first big speech for her when the Reagans were going to Ireland in June 1984. Nancy's father, Dr. Loyal Davis, was being posthumously inducted into the Royal College of Surgeons at University College Galway. They would be unveiling his portrait.

I met with her and she told me a lot of her memories of her dad that I could use in the speech. Just before I left the room to go to my computer and get busy, she said, "Please don't make me cry." (He had recently passed away.) Well, there was absolutely no way to fulfill her request. She adored him, that was clear. And speaking in tribute of him was bound to be emotional. So I just wrote it as she had told it to me in our meeting. Far from keeping the emotion out, I put it ALL in. Why? Because it was impossible not to under the circumstances and I knew it would make a better speech.

It was a success. Later, she told me that I totally captured him and it meant so much to her.

22

The Long Goodbye

Sunset and evening star
  And one clear call for me!
And may there be no moaning of the bar
  When I put out to sea;
But such a tide as moving seems asleep
  Too full for sound and foam
When that which drew from out the boundless deep
. *Turns again home*

Twilight and evening bell,
  And after that the dark!
And may there be no sadness of farewell
  When I embark;

For tho' from out our bourne of Time and Place
  The flood may bear me far,
I hope to see my Pilot face to face
  When I have crost the bar.

—Alfred Lord Tennyson (1889), "Crossing the Bar"

There are so many wonderful stories about Ronald Reagan; he had a marvelous sense of humor; he was truly humble and thoughtful.

He also had a real love of nature and nature's creatures. He never cut down a living tree, only branches blocking trails in the mountainous property around Rancho del Cielo. And he used everything he cut for fires on cold nights.

He collected acorns, which he left every morning outside his Oval Office door; the squirrels had come to expect breakfast on time and they could be insistent. If he was out of town, he made sure his secretary put out the acorns.

He doodled in meetings when he was bored. And he wasn't a bad caricaturist. He favored drawing horses' heads and cowboys.

And did he ever love good jokes.

I suspect he also had a stubborn streak. For one thing, he had a plaid suit that the photographers referred to as "the horse blanket." They hated it because it did not photograph well. He was well aware of their feelings, but he continued to wear it because he really liked it.

Our advance man Marty Coyne told the story that he once got a call from the FBI saying they wanted to interview him about Mike Deaver. This was after Mike had left the White House and started a very high-profile government relations firm with Bill Sittman, a former aide.

Marty had no idea why they wanted to talk to him but he felt he should tell Nancy about this development; she never liked surprises. He went up to the residence and told her; she immediately insisted on bringing the president in to hear this information. President Reagan listened to Marty recount his concern and here's what he said when Marty had finished: "Marty, always tell the truth."

It turned out to be nothing. But Marty said the president's guidance—"Marty, always tell the truth"—has stayed with him ever since. He now has grandchildren to whom he will pass that lesson.

I had an experience with President Reagan that stands out in my memory. I went upstairs to the residence to accompany Nancy to some event, long lost to memory. She was running late but the president came out into the living room and told me a story.

He said he'd just met the most impressive woman. She was from Chicago. She had lived in Nazi Germany and had sheltered a Jewish girl until she could get out of the country. They had just been reunited by a radio station in Chicago, if my memory serves. I could tell he was moved by the experience and I clearly remember thinking how wonderful it was that the man who was our president, with incredible power and influence, could still feel awe and amazement at the courage of this woman. It was almost as if he simply had to talk to someone about it and I was the first person in his line of sight.

Ed Hickey ran the White House Military Office just down the hall from the East Wing offices for Nancy's staff. Ed was a big, fun-loving Irishman who hosted an annual St. Paddy's Day celebration in his office. Tip O'Neill and Ronald Reagan always attended and the Irish jokes never stopped. Ed always invited the East Wing staff and we always went. Wouldn't miss it! There was nothing better than watching the president and the Speaker try to outdo each other with Irish humor. Sadly, Ed died of a heart attack at the young age of fifty-two. But I can just picture Ed and the president managing to find Tip O'Neill at that celestial party every St. Patrick's Day so the three of them could tell the newest "heavenly" jokes. Come to think of it, perhaps St. Patrick himself might join them.

The president occasionally arrived back in the family residence while we were still meeting with Nancy. I recall one such time when he walked into her office with his arms overflowing with boxes and bags. It seems these were items recently released by the White House Gift Office—where every gift given to anyone working at the White House from the president on down was appraised, logged in, and returned to the recipient with guidance. For employees, if the gift had a value of less than $100, it could be retained; if it was more valuable, it had to be returned. As I recall the president explaining all this to Nancy, they were allowed to keep the current batch of gifts in the private residence because they were all engraved and personalized, but when he left office they were required to be transferred to his library in California.

One time Nancy's phone rang when I was meeting with her, and the president walked in just as she answered the call. It was Billy Graham looking for the president. I can still see him sitting down in her desk chair, sliding it back away from the desk, and putting his feet up on the desk. They talked for at least fifteen minutes while Nancy moved over to her couch and we went back to whatever we were meeting about. She didn't even seem to object to his feet being on her desk. I suspect it wasn't the first time.

But even if there was no phone call or no gifts to share with

Nancy, Ronald Reagan always came directly to find her wherever she was as soon as he came back to the residence.

And then, in the blink of an eye, fifteen years later, she lost him.

* * *

We knew it was coming. Alzheimer's always ends in death, usually because of pneumonia. He died on June 5, 2004, fifteen years after leaving office—what Nancy called "the long goodbye."

After President Reagan released his moving letter, telling his "fellow Americans" about his recent medical diagnosis of Alzheimer's, Nancy's world gradually shrunk as the president's disease progressed. She almost never left their home, except for occasional lunches with friends. She told me about walking up the road to have lunch with Ursula, widow of Robert Taylor, every Saturday.

One day she called me at my Washington office to ask my advice. John Kennedy Jr. was starting his new magazine, *George.* He wanted to send a well-known photographer to Los Angeles to photograph President Reagan as the major focus for a piece on Alzheimer's.

Nancy was very fond of young John Kennedy and was torn about what to do. It would be a dramatic way to educate people about the disease. She simply asked me, "What should I do?" I reflected for a minute and said this, straight from my heart, "If the situation were reversed and he was being asked to allow you to be photographed, what would you want him to do?" She paused about five seconds and made up her mind. "You're right. I need to protect him. I will tell John no."

It is ironic that the same protectiveness she exhibited during the White House years that was a source of much press criticism became a virtue for the press to celebrate in these later years as she protected her failing husband. Nancy hadn't changed. Nancy was always just being Nancy.

Thanks to Nancy, when the time came, everything and everyone was in place; we knew our jobs. I was to take care of media needs during the days leading up to and during the funeral. Mike Deaver, then at Edelman Public Relations, and I met regularly to make sure we had everything covered. The wire services duly published the photos the First Lady had given me years before, her favorites. She'd asked me to encourage the media to use them when the time came. They were wonderful in honoring that request. Joanne Drake at the Ronald Reagan Presidential Foundation and Institute deftly handled media needs while the president's body lay in state at the library; I organized broadcast interviews for former senior staffers from our administration; days of nonstop interviews began.

While President Reagan lay in state at his library before being flown to Washington, the mourners never stopped coming to pay respects.

Nancy told me she was surprised by how many people came out and lined Pennsylvania Avenue as the funeral procession moved slowly toward the west steps of the Capitol. It was an amazing turnout. I asked her why she was surprised and she said, "I thought most people would have forgotten him after so many years." She was so wrong. Ronald Reagan, forgotten? Never.

I was standing in the Speaker's Office with Margaret Thatcher as Nancy walked with the casket up those steps to bring her husband to the rotunda where he would lie in state.

Mrs. Thatcher watched the air force jets roar across the sky as one plane fell away in the "Missing Man Formation." She turned to me and said, "You Americans have such wonderful traditions." I responded, "We probably stole them from you." She also told me that ever since President Reagan (Ronnie to her) had called many years before—at least twenty—and asked her to agree to speak at his funeral, she never traveled without packing a black suit because she always wanted to be ready to keep her commitment no matter where in the world she found herself. Is it any wonder why President Reagan held Maggie in such high regard?

The funeral at the National Cathedral on June 11 was a mixture of grief and pride. Everyone there had personal relationships with the Reagans and one another. President Reagan, the lover of Irish jokes and traditions, would have been proud of all the stories swapped while friends stood in the center aisle of that magnificent cathedral.

It resembled an Irish wake. There were plenty of hugs and tears and lumps in the throat—but there were smiles as well, because we all knew he was in the arms of the Lord.

Whenever I despair over what passes for journalism today, I remind myself that when it is really important, the press rises to the occasion. I just reread *Newsweek*'s June 21, 2004, issue covering President Reagan's funeral and Nancy's dignified presence. Its majestic photography caught the nation's mood; young people standing along Pennsylvania Avenue with watery eyes next to a military veteran saluting the presidential caisson; Nancy protectively walking with the casket toward the Capitol and later that night, at sunset, collapsing to kiss the casket as it moved into the crypt at the Reagan Library. Their daughter, Patti, wrote a column for the same issue of *Newsweek* about her father's faith that "God has a plan" and her belief that her mother will "find new life."

Most of that issue of *Newsweek* was devoted to President Reagan and Nancy and her passionate belief in stem-cell research as a potential cure for Alzheimer's. It also carried recollections from former President George H.W. Bush (41); Dennis LeBlanc, one of the president's dearest friends; actor Kirk Douglas; and Hollywood producer and Reagan friend, A. C. Lyles.

I look back upon my experience with the White House press corps fondly. Of course, we had just three networks—CNN was just getting started—two wire services, and a handful of major newspapers to deal with. No talk radio; no internet; no cell phones. Life was simple then, although it didn't feel that way at the time.

And I cannot tell you how much pride we felt at the dignity and courage of Nancy who had suffered along with him for so many years. According to the plans they made while he was still in office (required of every president), President Reagan's body was flown back to his library in Simi Valley where he was laid to rest in a tomb that faced west to the mountains just as the sun was setting. It held a place for his widow next to him. She would join him a few months short of twelve years later.

Years earlier, Nancy showed me his funeral plans. There, in his own hand, was the request that Alfred Lord Tennyson's poem "Crossing the Bar" be part of his service.

Nancy called me shortly after President Reagan's funeral and she told me that the thing she dreaded most was the idea of walking back into their empty house alone after the final service at the library. She didn't have to worry. Her two children, Ron and Patti, ordered pizza and went back to the house with her. They sat in the kitchen and talked while they ate. She said "It made all the difference."

It was hard not to worry about my friend who said her life didn't really begin until she met Ronald Reagan. When I visited her on one occasion after she was widowed, I saw a much physically diminished woman, holding on to the wall as she came down the hall because she'd broken her pelvis when she fell getting out of bed in the middle of the night. She told me she also had glaucoma. But when she sat down next to me and started showing me things, it was the same old Nancy. She didn't dwell on her limitations; she was very interested in what good stories I had to share, as always, from our nation's capital.

She talked about her Ronnie with pleasure evident in her eyes. She complained about how fat her dog was. While we were sitting there she seemed no older than she was when she was First Lady. We talked about her friends like Betsy Bloomingdale, whose bright, happy personality always made it fun to be around her. I left thinking Nancy's life, while limited by her physical challenges, was still satisfying for her.

But even then it was clear she did not fear the end of life because it would mean she would be reunited with her husband and that was the essence of her life.

It was just a matter of crossing the bar.

No Words

I cannot find the right words to bring you to the last pages of this book because they center on the death of Nancy Reagan on March 6, 2016.

She had so many loyal friends who tried to keep her busy and engaged. But there was one among the many whom I want to tell you about as we bid Nancy goodbye.

In the days leading up to her death, there was a tiny dog named Digby who'd brought her real comfort. Digby fit into the pocket of his owner, Robert Higdon. Robert and Nancy had become close friends over the years. Robert, a board member of the Ronald Reagan Presidential Foundation and Institute, had headed up the Prince Charles Charitable Foundation in the United States for many years and, more important, he is a wonderful human being and great company. Nancy truly adored him.

Robert and Digby spent many of those last days sitting by Nancy as she "slipped the surly bonds of earth." On their last visit, just a few days before Nancy died, Digby insisted on curling up on Nancy as she alternated between sleeping and waking. At one point Digby, who weighed only a few ounces, began to walk down from Nancy's abdomen toward her "lower regions," according to Robert. Nancy suddenly said, clear as a bell, "That better be Digby."

Nancy died quietly just days after putting Digby on notice. I like to think of that last encounter because it makes me smile. Nancy did have a wonderful sense of humor and that was one of the best examples I have. We who grieved her loss were also becalmed by the knowledge that she died peacefully in her sleep and that she was finally where she wanted most to be . . . with her Ronnie.

But still, several years later, it makes me sad to think that I will never pick up the phone and hear her voice again. In fact, knowing her—remember, she was relentless—maybe she'll work out a way to get a celestial phone installed. She knows my number.

Acknowledgments

To Clay Carson, USC student, who took on the poorly paid assignment of looking through boxes of materials at the Reagan Library for me. He unearthed a lot of helpful material. He worked closely with archivist Jennifer Mandel who was generous with her time and assistance. And, of course, my great thanks to Joanne Drake, chief administrative officer of the Ronald Reagan Presidential Foundation and Institute, for all her assistance.

To Kimberley Beckelman, my favorite hairdresser, for her brainstorm that resulted in the title of this book: *Lady in Red.*

To Jannie Giles for keeping our household in order and for the time she spent overnight to care for my dog while we traveled. She was a godsend.

This book really belongs to all my wonderful friends across the country who weighed in with memories. The experience of reconnecting with so many old Reagan alumni alone was worth the work.

To Toni Lynch Macpherson, a college friend from Pittsburgh, who helped me find Dr. Tom Starzl's email address.

To my friend Michie Bright who sent me information about the friendship between Nancy and Jehan Sadat. To Marcia Chipperfield, who was a big help in photographing some material for the book.

To Mark Weinberg who knows where to find anything and everything. And still has the best sense of humor of anyone, except the president, in the Reagan administration.

To Anne, Moni, Cookie, and Madge, the other members of the Fab Five of Falls Church (VA). High school friends who are simply the best. Thanks for giving me an excuse to push away from the computer on occasion and enjoy your company.

Many thanks to Dave Manzel, my daughter's father-in-law, for introducing me to his flying buddies who were retired crew members from Air Force One.

And to the members of my Literati and Farmington Book Clubs who have been patient about my prolonged absence. There is something ironic about not being able to read the book club selection because you are writing a book.

From start to finish, I appreciated the help and guidance from both Matt Lattimer and Keith Urbahn, my literary agents, and Mary Reynics, my editor at Crown. They answered every silly question I had. And demonstrated extraordinary patience!

And to everyone I forgot to mention. I will remember you in the middle of the night.

Photograph Credits